Remembering Kensington & Fishtown

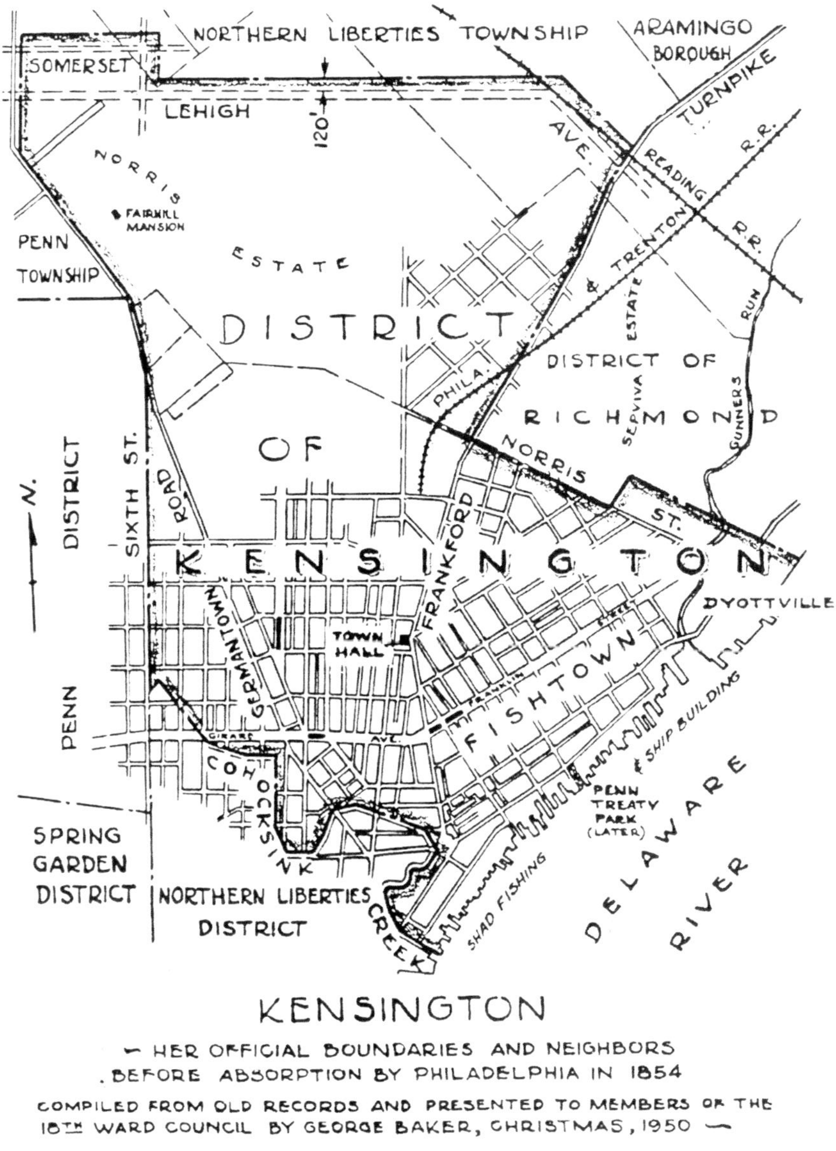

Kensington, her official boundaries and neighbors before absorption by Philadelphia in 1854. *Compiled by George Baker, 1950.*

REMEMBERING KENSINGTON & FISHTOWN

PHILADELPHIA'S RIVERWARD NEIGHBORHOODS

KENNETH W. MILANO

THE History PRESS

Published by The History Press
Charleston, SC 29403
www.historypress.net

All images are from the author's collection unless otherwise noted.

First published 2008
Second printing 2008
Third printing 2011

Manufactured in the United States

ISBN 978.1.59629.448.6

Library of Congress Cataloging-in-Publication Data

Milano, Kenneth W.
Remembering Kensington & Fishtown : Philadelphia's riverward neighborhoods / Kenneth W. Milano.
p. cm.
Includes bibliographical references.
ISBN 978-1-59629-448-6
1. Kensington (Philadelphia, Pa.)--History. 2. Fishtown (Philadelphia, Pa.)--History. 3. Philadelphia (Pa.)--History. I. Title. II. Title: Remembering Fishtown and Kensington.
F158.68.K46M55 2008
974.8'11--dc22
2008004623

Notice: The information in this book is true and complete to the best of our knowledge. It is offered without guarantee on the part of the author or The History Press. The author and The History Press disclaim all liability in connection with the use of this book.

For my wife Dorina—without her, nothing would get done. And for my boys, Francesco and Salvatore, who sacrificed their time with Daddy so he could pen these stories for our neighbors.

CONTENTS

FOREWORD

As a newspaper editor, I am always on the lookout for the big story. The things that happen in our world, how these events affect people and who the driving force is behind it all—these are the thoughts that consume my day. Luckily, as editor of *Star Newspapers*, there is never a lack of things to contemplate.

With real estate prices at an all-time high, a potential casino on the horizon, crime, politics and the never-ending threat of urban decay, it seems it's never hard to find that big story in Philadelphia's riverwards, the area we cover.

It can be very easy to get stuck in the present. With so much happening around us, sometimes the past gets lost in the shuffle. But as you're about to learn in the following pages of this book, the past is just as big of a story around here as the present.

As you will read, much has changed over the years. Roads now cover wagon trails, railroad tracks and where bodies of water once ran. Shopping complexes have been built on what was once farmland. A casino is proposed to be built on land that was once a British fort during the American Revolution. But as much as the area has changed over the past few centuries, it has stayed the same in one important way: the same working-class folk that founded the communities and that made the riverward neighborhoods grand so many years ago are the same types that grace the pages of the *Star* today.

So when local historian Ken Milano pitched the idea of a weekly column about the history of the neighborhoods, I knew I'd once again found that thing I am always seeking: the big story. With the neighborhoods once again in flux, now is the perfect time to document our past.

The people of the riverwards—longtime residents and newcomers alike—deserve to know their past. Because beyond the soaring skyscrapers and posh business districts, lies the heart of every great city. Here in Philadelphia, you can find that beating heart in the neighborhoods that make up the riverwards—Kensington, Port Richmond, Fishtown and Bridesburg.

In order to do the meticulous research necessary to put together the collection of columns that have been compiled for this book, one must have a true love for the work. It takes a man with patience, great knowledge and, most importantly, a heart the size of the neighborhoods themselves to trace this history. With "The Rest Is History," Ken's weekly column in the *Star*, he has done just that and more.

The author touches on such topics as the actual origin of the name "Fishtown"; Hope Farm and the founding of Port Richmond; the history of local cemeteries and playgrounds; important groups and people from throughout the area's history; and a plethora of other compelling subjects.

Both longtime residents and newcomers have come to cherish their weekly dose of "The Rest Is History." And now, in this book, you'll get a taste of some of Mr. Milano's finest work.

The history of a neighborhood plays a vital part in the identity of its residents. If you have lived in the neighborhood for many years, this book will be a heartfelt reminder of days gone by. If you have just come to call the area home, it is a way to learn more about the community you have joined. If you are not yet familiar with Philadelphia's riverward neighborhoods, start reading and I think you may find it hard to stop. Whatever the case may be, I hope you enjoy this collection of "The Rest Is History" columns as much as I have.

Ryan Smith
Editor, *Star Newspapers*

PREFACE

In February of 2006, Star Publications, the publisher for several community papers distributed in Philadelphia's riverward neighborhoods, began publishing a local history column titled, "The Rest Is History." This column was the first time a neighborhood newspaper dedicated a weekly column to the history of these ancient communities.

Most of the history columns in this book are about the history of Kensington, a town founded in the 1730s and self-governing between the years 1820 to 1854, before it was incorporated into the City of Philadelphia in 1854.

Occasionally, these articles will stretch over the very regulated (by the neighbors) borders to include the adjacent neighborhoods of Port Richmond and Northern Liberties. Since most of these stories deal with the olden days of Kensington, Fishtown (a later sub-neighborhood within Kensington) is referred to by its original name of Kensington on many occasions throughout the book.

In 1995, Dr. Harry Silcox, then director of the Institute for Service Learning, coordinated a project that included local school children interviewing senior citizens on the history of the Kensington neighborhood. During this exercise, Dr. Silcox was able to connect local historians Torben Jenk, Rich Remer and myself, three individuals who had been independently researching the history of the Kensington community. Torben, Rich and I helped Dr. Silcox to write the factual history of the community for his project, which provided the framework for the placement of the oral histories of the students and seniors. From this project, the book *Kensington History: Stories and Memories* was born in April 1996.

After the publication of this collaborative effort, Torben, Rich and I continued to meet to discuss the history of Kensington. Out of these meetings was born the Kensington History Project, an informal organization that researches, lectures and publishes on the history of Kensington and Fishtown, in addition to leading tours of the communities for interested souls and students. This book is another effort of the Kensington History Project.

I would like to thank Torben Jenk for reviewing the images chosen for this book and for supplementing them with images from his collection. Also, thanks goes out to Rich Remer who, by reading and critiquing this manuscript, helped to make it a better book. All faults of this book belong to the author.

PART I

OLDEN DAYS OF KENSINGTON

LENNI-LENAPE

ORIGINAL INHABITANTS OF SHACKAMAXON

Today, it is hard to imagine that our neighborhood once was the homeland of the Lenni-Lenape tribe of American Indians. No doubt there are still people in the area who can trace their ancestry back to the Lenape people. Recently I had a potential client call me from Florida, asking me to help her trace her Native American heritage. She grew up in Kensington, and in the process of tracing her family's history, she found evidence that her ancestors were Lenni-Lenape and had apparently never moved out of the area. And there I was, thinking it was neat that you could still find original eighteenth-century English and German families living in Kensington!

Over the years, the Lenni-Lenape people came to be known as Delaware Indians, having been given the name because they lived along the Delaware River. Englishman Samuel Argall is credited with giving the name Delaware to the Delaware Bay, in honor of Sir Thomas West, Third Lord de la Warr and onetime governor of Virginia Colony. Since the Delaware River fed the bay, it too was given the name of Delaware.

The Lenape homeland stretched from southeastern New York to northern Delaware State and from the Atlantic Ocean to the eastern woodlands of Pennsylvania. They were actually made up of three different tribes—the Munsee, the Unami and the Nanticoke. The Munsee inhabited the northern area, the Nanticoke the southern area and the Unami the middle area.

Hale C. Sipe, who studied the Delaware Indians, states that the Unami, or "downriver people," dwelled on both sides of the Delaware River, from the mouth of the Lehigh in the north to the Pennsylvania-Delaware border to the south.

Within the three tribes of Lenape there were also three clans. Those clans were the Turtle, Wolf and Turkey. The Turtle clan was the most important clan and always had the head sachem, or chief position, in any tribal council. The most important settlement of the Unami's Turtle clan was Shackamaxon, the place where the Philadelphia neighborhoods of Fishtown, Kensington and Port Richmond were later founded. Sipe theorizes that Shackamaxon was the capital of the whole Lenni-Lenape nation as, according to history and tradition, it was the principal settlement of the Unami tribe and their sachem was the leader of the united Lenape nation.

It should not be surprising, then, that William Penn, upon founding his colony of Pennsylvania, would come to Shackamaxon to make his peace treaty with the Native Americans—it was the chief village of the Lenape and the home of Tamanend, William Penn's counterpart for the American

Indians. Tamanend was sachem of the Turtle clan of the Unami, a position he held from sometime before Penn's arrival to at least 1697. He died about 1701 and is believed to be buried in the Tammany Burial Ground, near Chalfonte, in Bucks County, Pennsylvania.

By the time William Penn arrived on the scene in the late seventeenth century, the Unami were at a low point in their history. The entire seventeenth century was fairly devastating to them. They had fought a number of wars with neighboring Native American tribes over who would control the trade with the Europeans. In addition, there were boundary disputes between tribes encroaching on each other's traditional hunting grounds, which previously had not been an issue, but now, with the rise of commercial hunting for trade with the Europeans, presented serious problems. By the time the Swedes founded their Delaware Valley colony in the 1630s, the Lenni-Lenape were already a subject people to the Susquehannock tribe and needed permission to sell land to the Swedes.

The fifteen years (1660–1675) leading up to Penn's arrival in 1682 were the worst for the Lenape. There were more wars, this time with the Iroquois, in which the Lenape had to fight for the Susquehannock, as well as further smallpox outbreaks. The final results were that the Lenape nation, once twenty thousand strong, fell to a low of about four thousand.

After Penn's colony got underway and the American nation was eventually born, the Lenape began a slow, 130-year migration west, where the majority of them finally found a home on reservations in Oklahoma and Ontario, Canada.

So, it was surprising to receive that phone call from Florida from the woman looking for her Native American ancestors in Philadelphia, as most Lenape had long since left the area. Her ancestors never went to a reservation, and over time they intermarried with German immigrants, blending in and becoming part of the great American melting pot.

The Swedish Settlement of Shackamaxon

Before there was Fishtown or Port Richmond, or even Kensington, there was Shackamaxon. Shackamaxon was a sixteen-hundred-acre plot with borders that stretched from the old Cohocksink Creek (today's Canal,

Laurel, Bodine and Cambridge Streets) on the south to the Frankford Creek on the north, and from the Delaware River on the east to a disputed western border. Its western border did have the westernmost branch of the Cohocksink Creek as its southwestern border and presumably Frankford Avenue as its northwestern border, but the central western border was less defined, as it was a property line and not a road or creek.

The name of Shackamaxon is said to mean "place where the chiefs meet." The mouth of Gunnar's Run, a creek that emptied into the Delaware River (near present-day Dyott Street), was an area where the local Lenni-Lenape tribes would come to fish and hunt in the summer months. It was here that the Native Americans' council would have been held. It is no coincidence, then, that William Penn held council here with the local Lenape leaders at the place called Penn Treaty Park today.

The first Europeans to own land and live in Shackamaxon were Swedish settlers who colonized the Delaware Valley for the king of Sweden in the 1630s. They lost their colony to the Dutch, and the Dutch, in turn, lost the colony to the English, and thus William Penn eventually came to own the land that would become Pennsylvania.

Property records show that six Swedish families patented the land that made up Shackamaxon. The names on the deed of 1676 were Lasse Cock, Eric Cock, Michael Nilsson Lyckan, Otto Ernest Cock, Gunnar Rambo and Peter Nilsson Lyckan.

Historian Dr. Peter Craig researches and writes on the early Swedes. He has written a small piece on Shackamaxon, in which he informs us of who actually lived at Shackamaxon in 1671, in those early years before William Penn arrived.

Gunnar Rambo was one inhabitant. He was the brother-in-law to Lasse Cock, who also lived at Shackamaxon. Lasse married Martha Ashman, and they had at least two children.

Craig also tells us that Lasse Cock was the nephew of Michael and Peter Nilsson Lyckan, brothers who joined Lasse at Shackamaxon. In a compiled genealogy of the Cock family, we find that Eric Cock and Lasse Cock were brothers. Eric also lived at Shackamaxon.

Lasse Cock sold his interest in Shackamaxon to Elizabeth Kinsey in 1676 and moved to Passyunk. Otto Ernest Cock, a relative of Lasse Cock and the Lyckans, never lived at Shackamaxon and appears to have given his share to the Lyckans. The Lyckans and Gunnar Rambo in turn gave some land to Jacob Young, the sexton of Gloria Dei (Old Swedes) Church.

When William Penn arrived in the 1680s, only the Lyckan families, Eric Cock's family and Gunnar Rambo's family, as well as the sexton Jacob Young's family, were living at Shackamaxon.

By the 1690s, Michael Lyckan and Eric Cock moved to West Jersey, and Gunnar Rambo moved to Upper Merion Township. Sexton Jacob Young died at Shackamaxon in 1682, as did Peter Lyckan in 1692.

The founding of William Penn's colony of Pennsylvania precipitated the outward movement by the old Swedish families. Penn offered good incentives for the old-time settlers to move because he wanted the land that they had originally settled, the land that would become Philadelphia.

People like Thomas Fairman, Samuel Carpenter, John Bowyer and Robert Turner show up as being landowners on a map of Shackamaxon that was compiled in 1681. The little settlement of Swedes at Shackamaxon was turning English.

Thomas Fairman, through his wife Elizabeth Kinsey, acquired three hundred acres of Shackamaxon from Lasse Cock. It was a portion of this plot that Anthony Palmer would eventually purchase and on which he would found his town of Kensington in the 1730s.

Samuel Carpenter acquired a hundred acres from Gunnar Rambo; his plot would eventually be acquired by Isaac Norris and become part of the Sepviva Plantation of the Norris family, or the present-day eastern half of the Thirty-first Ward.

The shipwright, John Bowyer, also acquired his hundred acres from Gunnar Rambo. Bowyer's plot was on the old creek that runs under today's Aramingo Avenue. The creek was appropriately named "Gunnar's Run" after the original owner, Gunnar Rambo, whose property bordered the creek. Bowyer is believed to have been the first shipwright in the area that would eventually become part of Kensington, a place that would go on to become world famous for its shipyards and shipbuilding.

DID WILLIAM PENN'S TREATY WITH THE LENNI-LENAPE TAKE PLACE?

A small school of modern historians, who seem to be bent on destroying any tradition that predates them, argue that Penn's Treaty with the Native Americans at Shackamaxon did not take place because there is no written evidence of the event. Over three hundred years of tradition and two full investigative committees on the subject do not seem to faze them, nor does the fact that a "Treaty of Amity and Friendship" need not be written down.

Some say if the treaty took place, it would have taken place at Upland (Chester, Pennsylvania), the first capital of the Pennsylvania colony, but most historians of the eighteenth and nineteenth centuries who wrote on the topic thought Penn would never have pursued a "Treaty of Amity" at a fortified place like Upland. This doesn't leave many other suitable places in the Delaware Valley at that time. Even though Upland was the original capital of Penn's colony, it is said that Penn's character would not have allowed him to meet with the Native Americans in that manner—to negotiate a treaty in a military setting, which Upland would have been.

Shackamaxon, on the other hand, was a well-known place, where the Native American chiefs of different tribes would meet for their own councils.

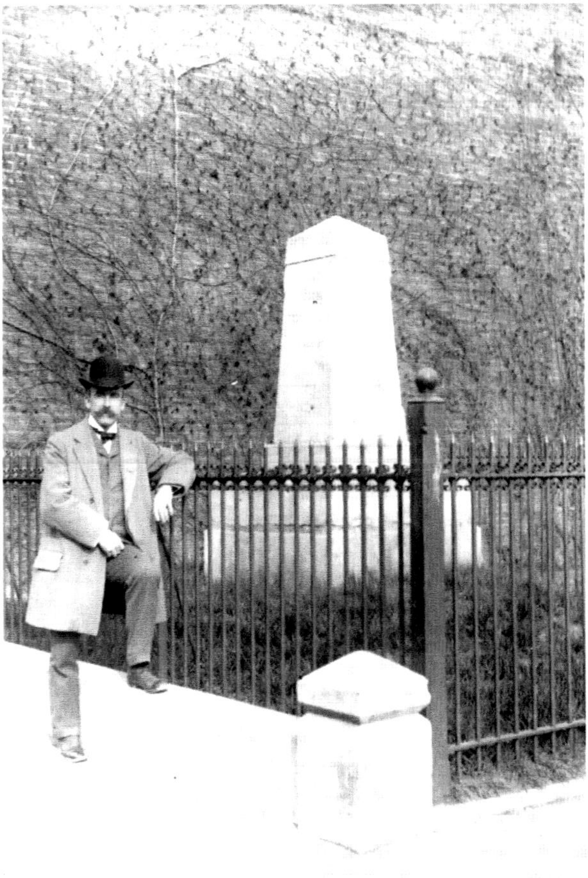

The Penn Treaty Monument in 1902, shown in its original location in the northwest corner of the park. Standing is W.H. Lawson.

It was also the place where Thomas Fairman, Penn's deputy surveyor, had built his home, entertained and put up the early arrivals of Penn's officers and council, people like William Markham (deputy governor), William Hague (land commissioner), Thomas Holme (surveyor general) and William Penn himself. Shackamaxon (Kensington) was an early headquarters of sorts for Penn's colony.

A long tradition, as evidenced by testimonies given to Roberts Vaux in 1825 by Judge Richard Peters (1744–1828) and David Conyngham, shows Shackamaxon to be the location of the treaty. Throughout their youths, Peters and Conyngham remember bathing on the shores of the sandy beach near the famous elm tree. The period of their youths would have been in the 1750s, and it was a known fact then that the "Treaty Elm" at Shackamaxon was the place of Penn's Treaty with the Native Americans—no one doubted it at that time. Additionally, Voltaire's famous quote on Penn's Treaty, a "treaty never written, never broken," was published in his *Dictionnaire Philosophique* in 1764. All of these events occurred before Benjamin West finished his famous painting of the treaty, a work said to have influenced the mysticism surrounding the event.

By looking at the background of Richard Peters, to see if he had credible knowledge of Penn's Treaty or was a person who would have been in a position to know something on the subject of the treaty tree, we find that he was a longtime judge for the United States District Court of Pennsylvania and a delegate to the Continental Congress in 1782–83. He was also the nephew of the Reverend Richard Peters (1704–1776), rector of Philadelphia's Christ Church. Judge Peters's time of bathing at the Treaty Elm would have been only sixty-five years or so after Penn's Treaty took place.

According to the testimonies, Benjamin Lay, the Quaker abolitionist who was born in 1681, pointed to the Treaty Elm and told Judge Peters and David Conyngham that this was the place where Penn had made his treaty with the Native Americans. Presumably, the aged Lay, who had settled in the Philadelphia area about 1732, when he was already in his fifties, would have talked with and known some of the folks who had been alive at the time of the treaty. It appears that, as early as the 1730s, the Treaty Elm was believed to be the site of the treaty.

The general acceptance of the Treaty Elm as the site of Penn's Treaty with the Native Americans is again shown in history by the actions that were taken by British General Simcoe. While quartering his men at Kensington (October 1777–June 1778) during the American Revolution, at the time of the British occupation of Philadelphia, Simcoe posted a sentinel at the Treaty Elm to keep it from being chopped down for firewood during that cold and difficult winter.

The living testimonies of Judge Peters and his friend Conyngham, their conversations with the aged Benjamin Lay, the actions of Simcoe and West's memorial painting, as well as the number of historians who recounted Penn's Treaty, all support the contention that the treaty indeed took place at Shackamaxon. In addition, the beliefs, customs and traditions of the local population of eighteenth- and nineteenth-century Kensington cannot be discounted. All of this evidence led the committee of the Historical Society of Pennsylvania that was investigating William Penn's Treaty to conclude that the treaty not only took place, but it took place at Shackamaxon.

HOPE FARM AND THE FOUNDING OF PORT RICHMOND

Many Fishtowners know that Anthony Palmer is credited with being the founder of Kensington, and we have Palmer Cemetery, Palmer Park and Palmer Street—all named in his honor. However, Palmer also played a large role in the founding of Port Richmond.

Palmer was a trader/merchant who came to Philadelphia via Barbados. He had been trading in Philadelphia as early as the 1690s. A fellow Barbadian, Captain George Lillington, owned a tract of land in Pennsylvania, which Anthony Palmer first purchased in 1704. Palmer paid Lillington five hundred Barbados pounds for the property. Captain Lillington acquired the property between 1697 and 1699.

In this three-year time period, Lillington purchased from several Swedish residents four continuous tracts of land situated on the Pennsylvania side of the Delaware River. The property was located north of the original city of Philadelphia in the area then known as Shackamaxon. The land he bought was roughly the area between today's Aramingo Avenue, Dyott Street (then a creek called Gunner's Run) and the Delaware River, with an undetermined northern border roughly following today's Allegheny Avenue.

These Swedes who held the land were the descendants of the original Swedish settlers, who had first colonized the Delaware Valley in 1634. The entire tract Palmer purchased, when combined, amounted to 582 acres, which was quite substantial. These sort of holdings were not easy to acquire in Palmer's Barbados. Besides the cost factor, the availability of large tracts of land in Barbados was unheard of and they were generally snapped up by the large planters.

There is no record of the exact date when Palmer first moved to Pennsylvania to take up residence, but by the year 1704 he owned property here and was starting to be considered one of the traders of note in the colony. It is clear that by the year 1709 he was a resident of Philadelphia County, as he is listed on a tax list for that year.

Palmer called the estate he acquired from Lillington "Hope Farm." He made Hope Farm his countryseat and this is where he lived for the next twenty-five years. During this period, Palmer enlarged his estate. To the 582 acres, which he acquired from Lillington, Palmer added an additional 27 acres when his friend John Tonk died in 1717. Palmer was one of three inheritors of Tonk's estate and he managed to buy out the other two. In 1729 Palmer added an additional 11 acres from Benjamin Fairman, the only surviving heir of Thomas Fairman. Thomas Fairman was an early large landowner who bought his property from the Swede Lasse Cock. Fairman was also the original owner of the Fairman Mansion, a property that Palmer eventually bought in 1729, and around which he built the town of Kensington, turning the Fairman estate into an early center of shipbuilding and fishing.

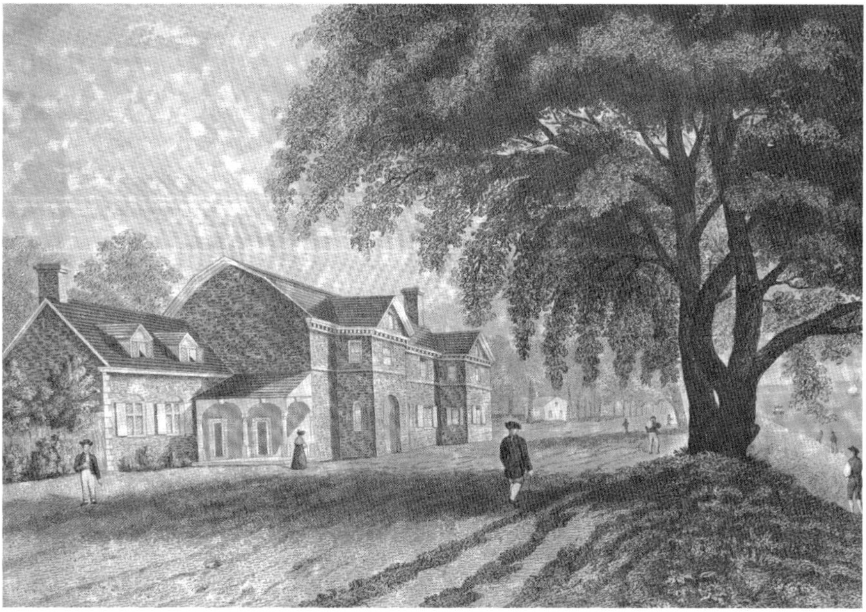

A nineteenth-century print of Fairman's Mansion and the Treaty Elm. Anthony Palmer bought the Fairman estate and founded Kensington there.

Eventually, Palmer acquired another 56 acres from Benjamin Fairman for his Hope Farm estate. These smaller acquisitions now gave Palmer a total estate of 676 acres. Palmer was finally reaching the landed gentry status that had eluded his father in Barbados.

During this time, Palmer may have begun to think of retiring from business. Records of his business dealings are almost nonexistent for this period. What records do exist lead one to believe that he was living the life of a propertied gentleman with a countryseat on a private plantation, an idea encouraged by William Penn when he founded the colony. Palmer joined a class of gentlemen including the likes of James Logan and Isaac Norris, both of whom had working plantations.

One thing that seems certain is that Palmer was beginning to mimic what Allen Tully calls "the customary English pattern of social mobility," which, over a couple of generations, "turned commercial wealth into land and a country seat."

In 1729 Palmer began the proceedings for selling Hope Farm. Palmer probably decided to give up Hope Farm when he found out that innkeeper Robert Worthington's property was coming up for sale. Worthington owned the much-desired Fairman Mansion estate. William Penn himself thought of acquiring the property in 1708. Penn's idea was to "live there out of the noise of Philadelphia but in sight of it."

The Fairman Mansion estate bordered on the south of Hope Farm, roughly the area bounded on the north by today's Aramingo Avenue and Dyott Street (then Gunner's Run), the Delaware River on the east, Columbia Avenue on the south and a western border comprising Frankford Avenue, Norris Street, Belgrade Street and York Street to Gunner's Run.

The Fairman Mansion was originally built and owned by Thomas Fairman, the assistant surveyor for William Penn. Fairman came into the property through his wife, Elizabeth Kinsey. At this time (in 1729), the Fairman estate comprised the mansion house, which was located at today's Penn Treaty Park, plus an additional 191.5 acres surrounding the home.

Palmer purchased the Fairman estate, and it was these 191.5 acres that he used to develop his town of Kensington by dividing it up into lots and selling to shipbuilders, who were eager for waterfront property. However, in order to finance his purchase of the Fairman estate, Palmer needed a buyer for his Hope Farm property.

The buyer Palmer found for the Hope Farm estate was William Ball. Ball was a local merchant who bought Hope Farm from Palmer in April of 1729 for the amount of £2,140 Pennsylvania currency. This represented a substantial profit for Palmer, since he had bought and inherited most of the estate for £500 Barbados currency. Along with the 676 acres of land, Ball acquired the messuage house, outhouses, orchard gardens, remaining rents and three slaves. The three slaves went along with the messuage house, and they were named Abraham, Hannibal and Phillis.

Palmer gave Ball six months to get the mortgage for the full amount, otherwise the property reverted back to Palmer. If Ball were to pay Palmer £1,000 sterling within six months, Palmer would allow this to count as £1,500 Pennsylvania currency.

It is assumed that William Ball was able to acquire a mortgage for Hope Farm in the allotted time period. The property never reverted back to Palmer. Ball built a mansion on the property near present-day Richmond and Cumberland Streets, calling it Richmond Hall after a suburb of London,

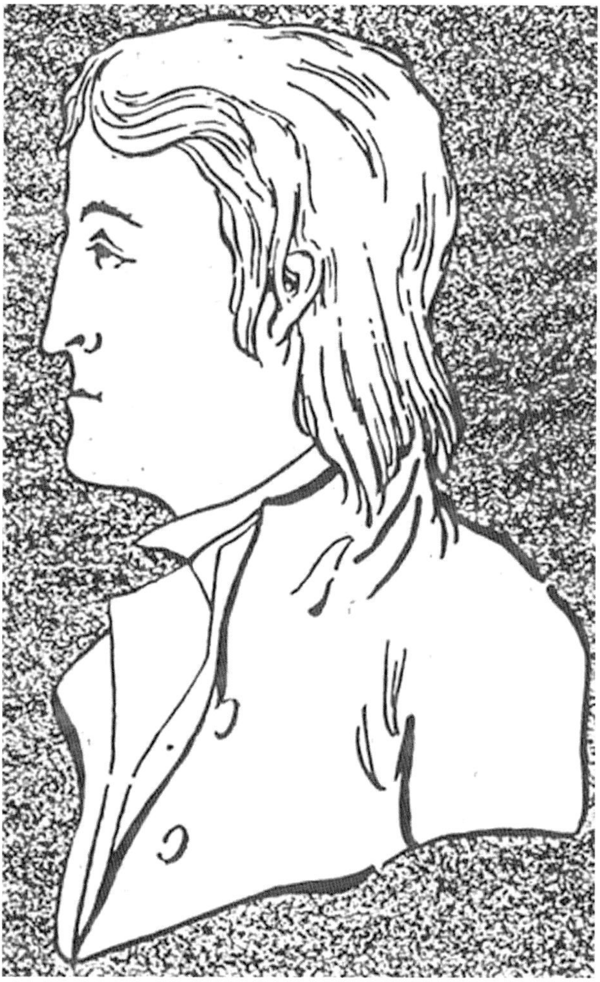

From his father, William Ball II inherited Hope Farm estate, which is most of the present-day neighborhood of Port Richmond.

similar to what Palmer did by renaming the Fairman estate Kensington after another London suburb of that time. Over time, the name of Hope Farm faded and Richmond came into use.

Using the money acquired from his sale of Hope Farm, in early January of 1730 Palmer paid cash to Robert Worthington for the former Fairman mansion estate. Along with the mansion house, the estate had the above-mentioned surrounding 191.5 acres that contained outhouses, stables, orchid gardens and a working plantation.

The Fairman mansion property was located directly south of Hope Farm on the Delaware River, or roughly today's Fishtown. Gunner's Run was the dividing line between Hope Farm and the Fairman property, which Palmer would soon rename Kensington.

The southeastern area of Hope Farm, near the meeting of Gunner's Run and the Delaware River, came to be known as Balltown. There were some manufactories established in Balltown by the time of the American Revolution, in particular a glassworks and calico printing works.

When William Ball died in 1740, he willed his property to his five children. Two of them took up the property, but the other three did not, since the land was not considered valuable on account of its swampy nature. Much of this land remained undeveloped from the time Ball died in 1740 until well into the early nineteenth century.

By the 1830s, the Philadelphia and Reading Railroad Company was looking around for property on the Delaware River to develop a "mine-to-ship" transportation system for the coal regions in upstate Pennsylvania. It was not easy finding open space on the Delaware River in the 1830s, particularly since there was tough competition for riverfront property from other railroads. The Philadelphia and Reading saw the swampy land of Hope Farm as just the place they wanted. The railroad purchased a large tract of land of the old Hope Farm estate along the Delaware River, above Cumberland Street. By the end of the 1830s the area began to be called Port Richmond, since it was now the main "port" for Pennsylvania's coal regions.

If it had not been for Anthony Palmer buying up properties and consolidating them into one huge estate, the future Port Richmond may not have had the large open spaces that the Reading Railroad needed. In his own way, Palmer can be considered one of the founders of today's Port Richmond.

THE BUILDING AND BREAKUP OF THE FAIRHILL ESTATE

When the Fairhill estate was incorporated into the District of Kensington in 1848, it brought the end to a 140-year history of one of Philadelphia's most famous colonial country estates. This column is too short to give the full history of the estate, but taking a peek at its building and breakup is most interesting.

The estate, at its largest, ran from today's Germantown Avenue on the west to Aramingo Avenue on the east, and from Norris Street on the south to slightly above Lehigh Avenue on the north. The estate consisted of two tracts: the Fairhill estate (the country home and garden of the Norris family), which was west of Frankford Avenue, and the Sepviva Plantation (the working farm), which was east of Frankford Avenue.

In 1709, Isaac Norris purchased from Arnold Cassell the first parcel of land that would become the Fairhill estate and the nucleus around which Fairhill was built. Cassell had acquired it from Andrew Robeson. The Cassell property was 156 acres and sat south of and contiguous to the Fairhill Meetinghouse, an old Quaker meeting located at what today would be Germantown and Cambria. This 156-acre property was part of two 80-acre plots of "liberty land" that belonged to first purchasers William Stanley and James Claypoole.

Andrew Robeson had purchased these separate eighty-acre liberty land plots from Stanley and Claypoole and consolidated them under one deed. The lots sat next to each other on the farthest reaches of the southern branch of Gunner's Run, an old creek that ran under today's Aramingo Avenue. The creek had a branch that meandered westward over toward Ninth and Lehigh. Norris apparently built his Fairhill Mansion on the Cassell property, situated roughly at today's 7th and York Streets.

William Penn, as an incentive to lure investors to his new colony, would give liberty land plots to those who purchased large pieces of property. Typically, a person would buy a large parcel of land in the hinterland and receive 1 percent of their acreage in liberty land; thus five thousand acres of hinterland would get you fifty acres of liberty land. Also included in the deal was a town lot in the city of Philadelphia. These liberty lands were located in what would become the "Northern Liberties." However, that would not be just the Northern Liberties neighborhood today, but actually it would cover everything in Philadelphia County north of Vine Street to the present-day city borders.

Many of these liberty land plots were never settled, or if they were, they were kept briefly as real estate investments and then, to use the jargon of today, "flipped" to make a quick profit. Isaac Norris purchased a number of these liberty land plots in the Northern Liberties and consolidated them under one deed to create the Fairhill estate and Sepviva Plantation.

Three years after first purchasing the Cassell property, Norris purchased the 470-acre estate of Samuel Carpenter. This estate made up roughly all of the Sepviva Plantation and had water frontage along Gunner's Run. Carpenter was a first purchaser who received liberty lands and consolidated them with various properties he bought from Gunner Rambo and some other liberty landholders.

As William Penn and the English moved in, the Swedes sold out and moved farther inland, or over to South Jersey. Carpenter bought lands from these Swedes and took out one patent for his various land purchases. He then sold the big acreage to Norris. Also during this period, Norris bought up another 198 acres of liberty lands and took out a patent on the whole estate, which now measured 824 acres.

The estate was beautifully laid out with a fine mansion house, a renowned garden and a working plantation. At this time, Frankford Road cut through the estate, giving Norris access to a north–south road to town or to the northeast parts of the county. The eastern edge of the Sepviva Plantation had water access from Gunner's Run, which was an easy boat ride to the Delaware and into town, providing alternative travel in the event of bad roads in the winter or rainy months. There was a road cut out from Gunner's Run to the Fairhill Mansion, which would appear to roughly parallel today's York Street. At the western edge, near Norris's mansion house at 7th and York Streets, was Germantown Road, which again allowed easy access into town as well as to Germantown and points northwest. Over all, Norris did pretty well for himself considering he had not arrived first!

The creator of the Fairhill estate had been Isaac Norris Sr. (1671–1735), a wealthy Quaker merchant. After his death in 1735, the estate was taken over by his son, also named Isaac Norris (1701–1766). Isaac Norris Sr.'s son Isaac is often called "the Speaker," not only to differentiate him from his father, but also because he was the Speaker of the general assembly of the Pennsylvania Colony.

Isaac Norris, the Speaker, died in 1766, and his only surviving daughter, Mary Norris, inherited her father's estate. Besides the large, eight-hundred-plus acres of land that the estate included (all of the current land from Germantown Avenue on the west to Aramingo Avenue on the east, and from Norris Street on the south to slightly above Lehigh Avenue on the north), there was also the Fairhill Mansion at what would today be 7th and

York Streets, as well as Mary Norris's very famous library, first established by her grandfather and then built upon by her father.

Mary Norris married John Dickinson (1732–1808) in 1770 and the couple lived at Fairhill. Through his marriage to Mary, Dickinson came into possession of the Norris library. During the American Revolution, the Fairhill Mansion was sacked and burned by the British, but Dickinson was able to save the library.

Dickinson is well known as the author of the famous work *Letters from a Farmer in Pennsylvania*, a treatise regarding the nonimportation and nonexportation agreements against Great Britain. He was a member of the Pennsylvania Assembly, and in 1775, with Thomas Jefferson, he wrote *Declaration of the Causes and Necessity of Taking Up Arms*. Ironically, Dickinson, who attended both Continental Congresses, did not sign the Declaration of Independence, as he did not want to break with England. Because of this, he is not as well known in history as Thomas Jefferson and the other founding fathers.

While the British may have destroyed Fairhill Mansion, Dickinson did salvage one of American's great colonial libraries. Upon the chartering of Dickinson College, his namesake institution, he donated the Norris library to the college. Today, the library, known as the Norris Collection, still exists. It is an amazing collection of sixteenth-, seventeenth- and eighteenth-century books, numbering near two thousand volumes. It was considered one of the finest libraries in colonial America in its day and represents one of about ten intact colonial libraries still in existence.

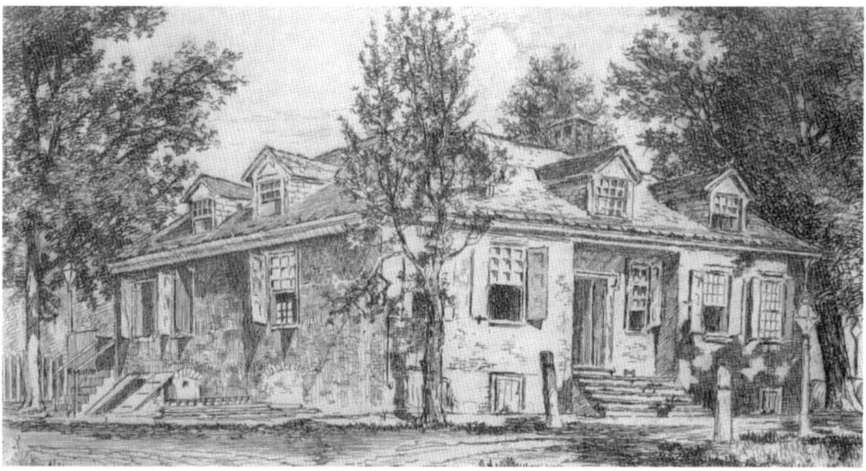

The rebuilt Fairhill Mansion, which was burned by the British during the Revolutionary War in 1777, was located near today's 7th and York Streets.

CATALOGUE

OF LOTS OF

FAIRHILL LAND CO.

The following is a description of all the Lots of the Company, except a few North of Clearfield Street and the angular Lots on the southern end of the property.

We give the sizes, valuation prices per foot, and cost of each Lot carried out.

A Plan may be seen at the Office, No. 204 South Fourth Street.

EAST SIDE OF SIXTH, A 50-FOOT STREET, BETWEEN CAMBRIA AND CLEARFIELD STS., THE VALUATION IS $2.00 PER FOOT.

(This street is paved and water-pipe laid.)

25 *Lots* 18 *feet front, by* 68 *feet* $10\frac{1}{2}$ *inches deep,*
at $2 *per foot, each costs* $600.00

4 *Lots* 17 *feet front by* 68 *feet* $10\frac{1}{2}$ *inches deep,*
at $2 *per foot, each costs* 566.67

1 *Lot* 17 *feet* $3\frac{1}{4}$ *inches front by* 68 *feet* $10\frac{1}{2}$ *inches deep,*
at $2 *per foot, costs* 575.68

WEST SIDE OF FAIRHILL, A 50-FOOT STREET, BETWEEN CAMBRIA AND CLEARFIELD STS., THE VALUATION IS $1.50 PER FOOT.

22 Lots 16 feet front by 68 feet deep,
at $1.50 per foot, each lot costs . . . $400.00

17 Lots 17 feet front by 68 feet deep,
at $1.50 per foot, each lot costs . . . 425.00

1 Lot 16 feet $3\frac{1}{4}$ inches front by 68 feet deep,
at $1.50 per foot, costs 406.78

1 Lot, 16 feet 5 inches front by 68 feet deep,
at $1.50 per foot, costs 410.42

Catalogue of the Fairhill Land Company, a company formed to sell off lots at the breakup of the Fairhill estate.

After Mary Norris's death, the estate went to Isaac Norris III, the eldest son of Mary's Uncle Charles Norris, and Charles's second son, Joseph Parker Norris. This agreement to give the property to her cousins was a condition that had previously been placed upon Mary by her father.

When Joseph Parker Norris died in 1841, he gave the larger piece of the estate (the Fairhill estate west of Frankford Avenue), about 498 acres, to his five sons, and the other part (the Sepviva Plantation, east of Frankford Avenue), about 155 acres plus the marshland around Gunner's Run, went to his six daughters.

After probating the will of Joseph Parker Norris, there were some legal entanglements that kept the estate in the courts for a while and thus held up development for a time. But by 1848, the trustees of the Fairhill estate allowed it to be incorporated into the then self-governing District of Kensington. The Fairhill estate nearly doubled the size of Kensington, as the northern border that used to sit on Norris Street between Frankford and 6th Streets was now moved north to Lehigh Avenue and the northwest corner went to Germantown and Lehigh Avenues.

The commissioners of Kensington began to lay out and grade the streets, while the Norris family's estate agents began selling off lots to potential developers. This large expanse of open land so near to the core of the city is the reason that Kensington became the base for many large manufacturers, as large lots of open land close to the city were not available elsewhere.

Before allowing Kensington to take over Fairhill, the Norris family insisted on laying aside land for public parks. Hence, today we still have Norris and Fairhill Squares. The Sepviva Plantation developed a little later, but by the time of the Civil War, this area too was being carved up with streets and lots were being sold. Thus, the old Norris family estate of Fairhill was no more.

PART II

EARLY INDUSTRY IN KENSINGTON AND FISHTOWN

EARLY GLASSMAKING IN KENSINGTON

In a letter written in 1683, William Penn mentioned that glass was being made in Pennsylvania. While he did not state where it was being made, a later record confirms that there was a glasswork at Shackamaxon, an old Swedish settlement that eventually evolved into Kensington.

While we do not have the exact location, this Shackamaxon glasswork was said to be "conveniently posted for water carriage," thus it must have been on the banks of the Delaware River, or Gunner's Run. In all probability, it was located on the north bank of Gunner's Run, the old creek that runs under Aramingo Avenue near the Delaware River, just east of where Dyott Street meets Beach Street.

It was on the north bank of Gunner's Run that several eighteenth-century glassworks were built, so we can assume that this late seventeenth-century glasswork would probably have been in the same area. We know that it wasn't north of this point, as it became fairly swampy between Gunner's Run and the Delaware River. Also, it is fairly certain that it would not have been located south of Gunner's Run, as the property of that area is well documented and there were no glassworks found.

This area on the north bank of Gunner's Run later took the name of Balltown, and there was some industry established there in early colonial times. The property belonged to William Ball, who had purchased the Hope Farm estate from Kensington founder Anthony Palmer about the year 1729. The Ball family rented out property to Robert Towars and Joseph Leacock, who built a glasshouse about 1771. Leacock was a cousin to Deborah Franklin, the wife of Benjamin Franklin. It is probable that it was to this Balltown family connection that Franklin looked when he was asked to help set up John Hewson in America. Hewson wound up setting up his calico printing works on the border of Balltown in the early 1770s. His printed fabrics were of a quality that rivaled the British and French productions of that period.

By the third decade of the nineteenth century, the name of the locale changed from Balltown to Dyottville, as it was here that the well-known glasswork of Dr. Thomas W. Dyott was established. The rows of two-and-a-half-story houses on the 1100 blocks of East Hewson and East Berks Streets, east of Girard Avenue, are relics of the homes built by Dyott for his glassworkers in the 1820s.

A large majority of the glass blowers employed by Dr. Dyott were Germans. He is said to have had a hundred glass blowers and two hundred apprentices, and he created a sort of utopian community where he had both a school and houses for his workers. In addition, he founded his own bank,

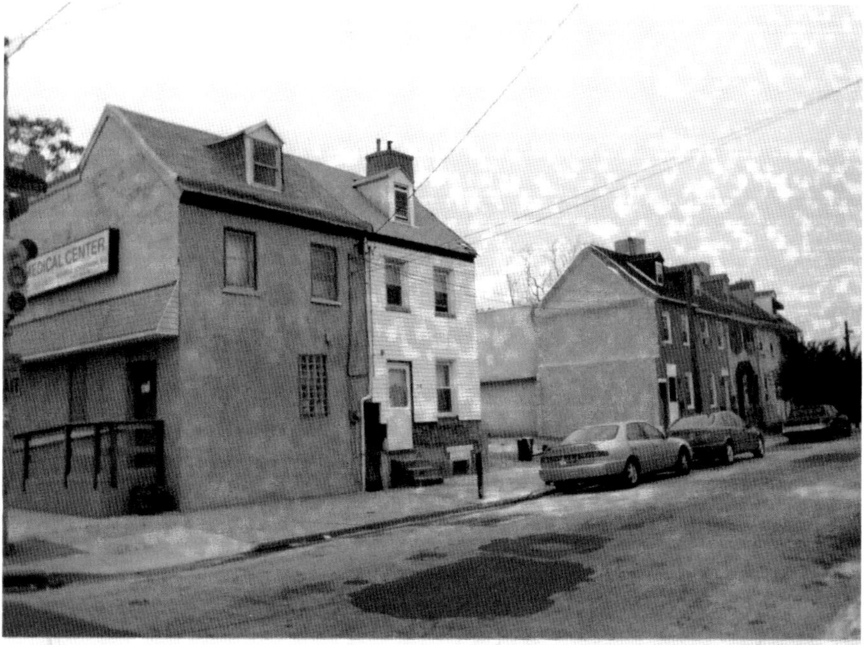

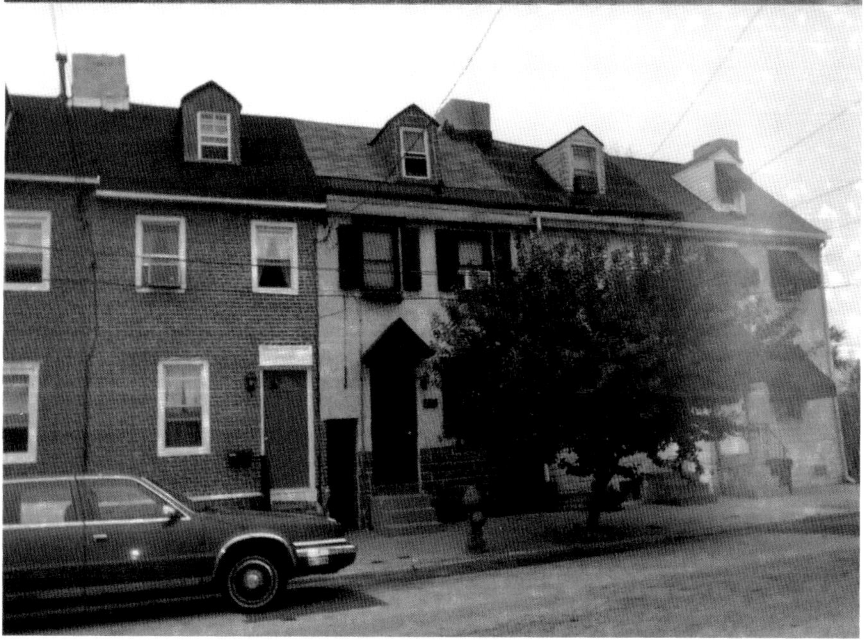

The 1100 block of East Berks Street, the last vestiges of Dyottville, built circa 1820s for the workers of Thomas W. Dyott's glasswork.

the Manual Labor Bank. However, the bank overextended its dealings and went bankrupt during the Panic of 1837.

German glass blowers in the employ of Caspar Wistar established eighteenth-century glassmaking in the Delaware Valley. Wistar, also German and a Philadelphia resident, had a fairly successful glasswork at Alloway, New Jersey, that he started about 1739. He made mostly window glass and bottles. The glasshouse finally closed about 1780, a casualty of the Revolutionary War.

Wistar helped to establish the German glassmaking tradition in the colonies. Another German, Henry William Stiegle, was next in line to follow Wistar. Stiegel is probably the most famous glassmaker of his age, being the founder of the Stiegel glasswork at Manheim, Pennsylvania.

What little evidence that exists for glassmaking in eighteenth-century Kensington comes in the form of advertisements that were run in eighteenth-century Philadelphia newspapers. George Bakeoven, whose family was one of the early fishermen families of Fishtown, advertised in August of 1777:

> *At a considerable expence,* [Bakeoven and Farrell] *brought to perfection the blowing of glass, and have now for Sale, at their warehouse in Kensington...Quart and Pint Decanters, Quart and Pint Tumblers, Wine Glasses, and Phials.*

Bakeoven's partner was an Irish immigrant named Felix Farrell. He is mentioned in a newspaper advertisement put out by Henry William Stiegle, the Manheim glassmaker, as having been an indentured servant who ran away from Stiegle in November 1771, only to turn up in Kensington in 1777. Farrell was described as "23 years of age, 5 feet 6 inches high, fair

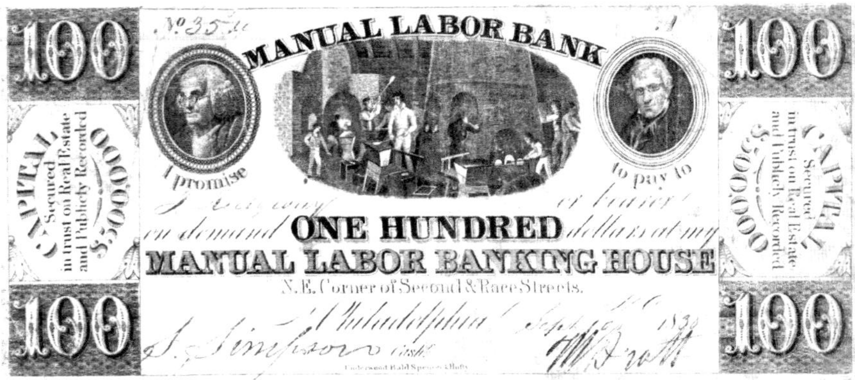

A hundred-dollar bill of Dyottville founder Thomas W. Dyott's Manual Labor Bank, dated September 10, 1838, several months before he went bankrupt.

complexion, brown hair, and has a remarkable scar on his face; had on a brown cloth coat, a striped jacket (part silk) and is very talkative."

Besides being eighteenth-century Kensington glassmakers, Bakeoven and Farrell also might be the earliest advertised recyclers in Kensington as well. In one of their advertisements dated August 27, 1777, they state that they "likewise give the best Price for old broken Glass such as Flint and Window Glass."

JOHN HEWSON

CALICO TEXTILE PRINTER AND REVOLUTIONARY WAR HERO

John Hewson was born in 1744 in England and was the son of a London woolen draper. He was a descendant of Colonel John Hewson, who was a supporter of Oliver Cromwell and was implicated in the execution of King Charles I. Like his famous ancestor, and to the dismay of his parents, young John Hewson held radical political views. Republican tendencies did not fare well under King George III, and Hewson's parents, with the help of that most famous of Philadelphians, Benjamin Franklin, were able to get young John to immigrate to America in 1774.

Hewson was trained as a printer of calico fabrics and had worked for Talwin and Foster, a leading English textile print works, at Bromley Hall near London. He very likely brought his equipment to Philadelphia, and perhaps half a dozen workmen as well. In 1774, he opened a calico-printing factory on the north bank of Gunner's Run, near the Delaware River. At that time, Richmond Street was called Point-No-Point Road, and Hewson's address was listed on Point Road. Today, Fishtown has a small street named Hewson, near the original location of his factory.

Not only was Hewson the first calico fabric printer in the colonies, but his work was also of the highest quality. According to Dr. Kimberly Wulfert, a textile historian, Hewson's textiles were unmatched in America at that time and rivaled those of Europe. His chintz fabrics made him famous and were "printed with wood blocks; a different one was used for each of the seven colors in his palette; pink, red, blue, yellow, black and brown. Green colors were added by 'pencilling' in blue and yellow dyes."

Wulfert adds that Hewson's textiles were

> *expensive and highly sought after for dresses, furnishing fabrics and handkerchiefs. He was most known for his realistic and finely detailed classical urns of flowers, which were printed as medallion panels for bedcovers, it is believed. Women sewed these square panels into the center of a quilt, surrounding it with many frames of floral garlands, or borders of pieced stars or triangles and squares. Bedcoverings could be made this way; 100" X 100" or larger, was a common size for quilts then.*

To make the coveted chintz panels go further,

> *women would cut out the birds, butterflies, flowers and other motifs. Using an appliqué stitch, the pieces were reapplied, spread apart onto a large plain background. Blank spaces were filled with less expensive chintz or calicos and intricate quilt patterns.*

Hewson is still considered one of the finest craftsmen in textile printing history.

In 1775, Martha Washington is said to have paid a visit to John Hewson at Kensington. William Ball, who owned the property on which Hewson's factory stood, was thought to be related to Mrs. Washington, whose maiden name was Ball. Mrs. Washington had heard of Hewson's fabrics and wanted to commission an image on a handkerchief depicting her husband on horseback. It is supposed that Mrs. Washington eventually became a patron and visitor of Hewson's calico printing factory.

At the outbreak of the American Revolution, John Hewson, already a vocal supporter of the Patriot cause, enrolled in the First Republican Grenadiers in 1775. After this group disbanded, he was commissioned as an officer, formed a company of men out of his factory workers and had himself attached to the county militia.

Hewson had to flee Philadelphia for New Jersey when the British invaded and occupied the city in 1777. British soldiers were quartered in a fort built in Kensington, and eventually the Brits sacked Hewson's office and factory. He narrowly escaped with some of his tools, machinery and animals by taking a boat off the Kensington shore just before the British arrived. Hewson was eventually captured in New Jersey, and after spending some time in the Walnut Street Prison, he was transferred to New York. After a brief imprisonment there, he managed to escape, almost drowning in the process.

When the Revolution ended, Hewson set about restoring his business. Due to his patriotism and daring escapes, he became a local war hero.

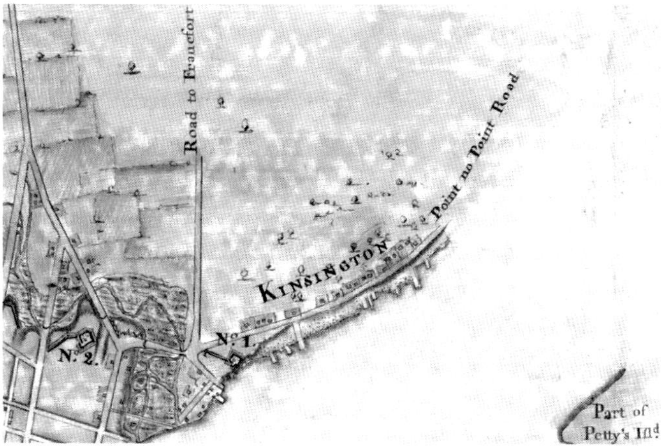

A map surveyed and drawn by Pierre Nicole, November 1777, showing British Fort (No. 1) located in Kensington. *Courtesy Library of Congress (LOC), Geography and Map Division.*

During the Grand Federal Procession on July 4, 1788, Hewson was honored in the parade, traveling at the center of the manufacturers' float.

In 1790 the Pennsylvania Manufacturing Society awarded Hewson a gold medal for the best example of calico printing in the state. He retired from his business in 1810 and helped to found Kensington Methodist Episcopal "Old Brick" Church. John Hewson, a true Kensington patriot, died in 1821 and is buried on the north side of the Palmer Cemetery, near the Montgomery Street gate.

Folk Art, the magazine of the American Folk Art Museum in New York, published a detailed article in the fall of 2007 by Dr. Kimberly Wulfert about John Hewson's textiles, illustrating in color a number of his creations.

THE FISHERMEN OF FISHTOWN

When the Lord made shad
The Devil was mad
For it seemed such a feast of delight
So to poison the scheme
He jumped in the stream
And stuck in the bones out of spite.
—An old fisherman's poem

Have you ever wondered why they call our neighborhood Fishtown? Rich Remer did, and he has spent a good deal of time researching the history of the Delaware River shad fishing industry, which was dominated and controlled by a group of families who had their roots and residences in that small area of Kensington that came to be known as Fishtown.

Remer is one of the founders (along with Torben Jenk and myself) of the Kensington History Project, a local group that researches, publishes and lectures on the history of Kensington and Fishtown. Remer has done a tremendous amount of research on the shad fishing of the early fishing families of Fishtown (try saying that ten times real fast).

According to Remer, shad was once the second most popular fish in the United States, after cod, and there was a time when the Delaware River was teeming with shad. The "Kensington shadders," as Remer calls them, were a tightknit group, often intermarrying and living in the same general neighborhood. This neighborhood was the original section of Kensington and had as its borders the old creek Gunner's Run on the north, the Delaware River on the east, Palmer Street on the south and roughly Moyer Street on the west. This small portion of Kensington became known as Fishtown because many of the Delaware River's fishermen lived here, married here and died here.

Remer discovered that over the course of the nineteenth century, the fishermen families of Fishtown had

> *gradually bought or leased the shore fisheries of the lower Delaware River estuary and by mid-century they controlled the catch. The neighborhood was called Fishtown because these families controlled the fishing; it was "the" home for fishermen, not just for Kensington, or Philadelphia, but the whole of the Delaware River and Bay.*

The surnames of these early fishermen stand out as beacons of the history of the community: Baker, Bakeoven, Bennett, Collar, Cramp, Faunce, Gosser, Pote, Rice, Shibe, Tees and Tuttle. Of these families, the main fishing families were the Bennetts, Cramps, Faunces, Gossers and Rices. Many of these families served or founded local social institutions and churches and played major roles in the development of Kensington's Fishtown section. Benjamin Shibe, the owner of the old Philadelphia Athletics baseball team, hailed from a Fishtown fishing family, as well as the great shipbuilding family of William Cramp. If you stroll through Palmer Cemetery (Memphis and Palmer Streets), you will see many of these early fishermen buried on the hill along the Memphis Street side.

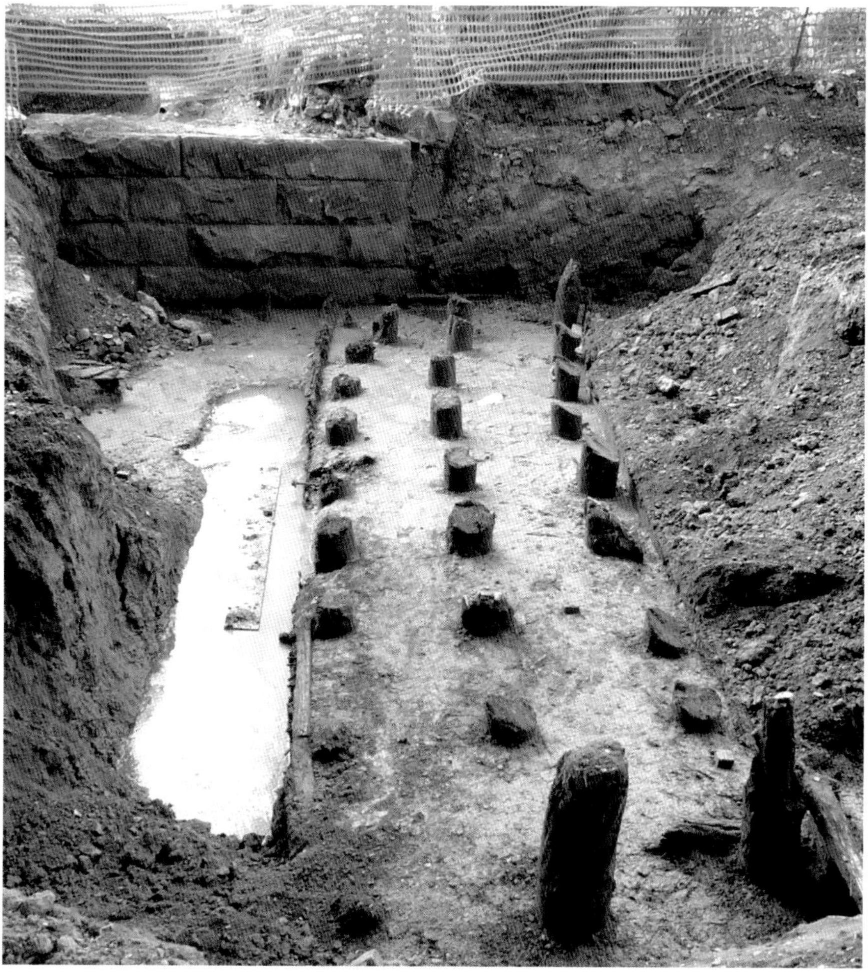

In 2007, archeologists found wood pilings and stone abutment, likely the bridge that carried Girard Avenue and Norris Street over Aramingo Canal. *Courtesy Torben Jenk.*

The foot of Susquehanna Avenue was the main dock for the fishermen, and it was here where you had a "veritable fish market with numerous skiffs and catboats." It would not be uncommon to see women with baskets of fish on their heads. "Purchasers would come to the wharf and make their purchases, the 'catties' and eels being skinned in their presence thus guaranteeing fresh fish." However, much of the selling of the fish was handled in town at the fish market on Dock Street.

Over time, the shad fisheries came to an end. Due to the combined pressures of "over fishing, pollution, and environmental degradation," Fishtown's fishermen left to find work elsewhere. A number of them had diverted their profits into local real estate; others went into that other popular neighborhood business of shipbuilding. Today, after "peaking in the early 1900s," Remer says that the Delaware River shad fishery has now dwindled to "one operating commercial establishment, the Lewis Fishery of Lambertville, New Jersey, and Fishtown's glorious shad seasons are forever gone."

John Harrison

America's First Industrial Chemist

John Harrison (1773–1833), considered by many to be America's first industrial chemist, was a resident of Kensington. Material on the years of his life while he lived in Kensington is hard to come by. However, there is a scarce genealogy of Harrison's family titled *Annals of the Ancestry of Charles Custis Harrison and Ellen Waln Harrison*, compiled by their daughter-in-law Mary Harrison.

John was a descendant of "Thomas Harrison, of Stoneraise, and Castle Sowerby, Cumberland County, England," who was born about 1640. Stoneraise is a parish about ten miles beyond Carlisle. Thomas Harrison was a follower of George Fox, a member of the Religious Society of Friends. Thomas had a son Thomas, who also had a son Thomas, and the fifth son of this third Thomas, born August 29, 1741, and also named Thomas, is the one from whom Kensington's John Harrison was descended. This Thomas Harrison applied to the Carlisle Monthly Meeting for a certificate of removal, and in the minutes entered at the monthly meeting at Carlisle for the "20th of 5th Mo. 1763," there was a certificate issued and given on behalf of Thomas Harrison. This certificate was directed to the Society of Friends in Philadelphia, the place to which Thomas Harrison immigrated.

Harrison, then only twenty-two, came to America and joined the Society of Friends in Philadelphia. Soon after, he married a young woman, who in "later years, was to become one of the most celebrated Quaker preachers of her day." The records of the Philadelphia Monthly Meeting show that

> *on Sixth Mo. 21, 1764, Thomas Harrison of Philadelphia, son of Thomas, deceased, of Thurston Field, Cumberland County, Great Britain, was married at the Philadelphia Meeting to Sarah Richards, daughter of Rowland Richards, deceased, of Chester County.*

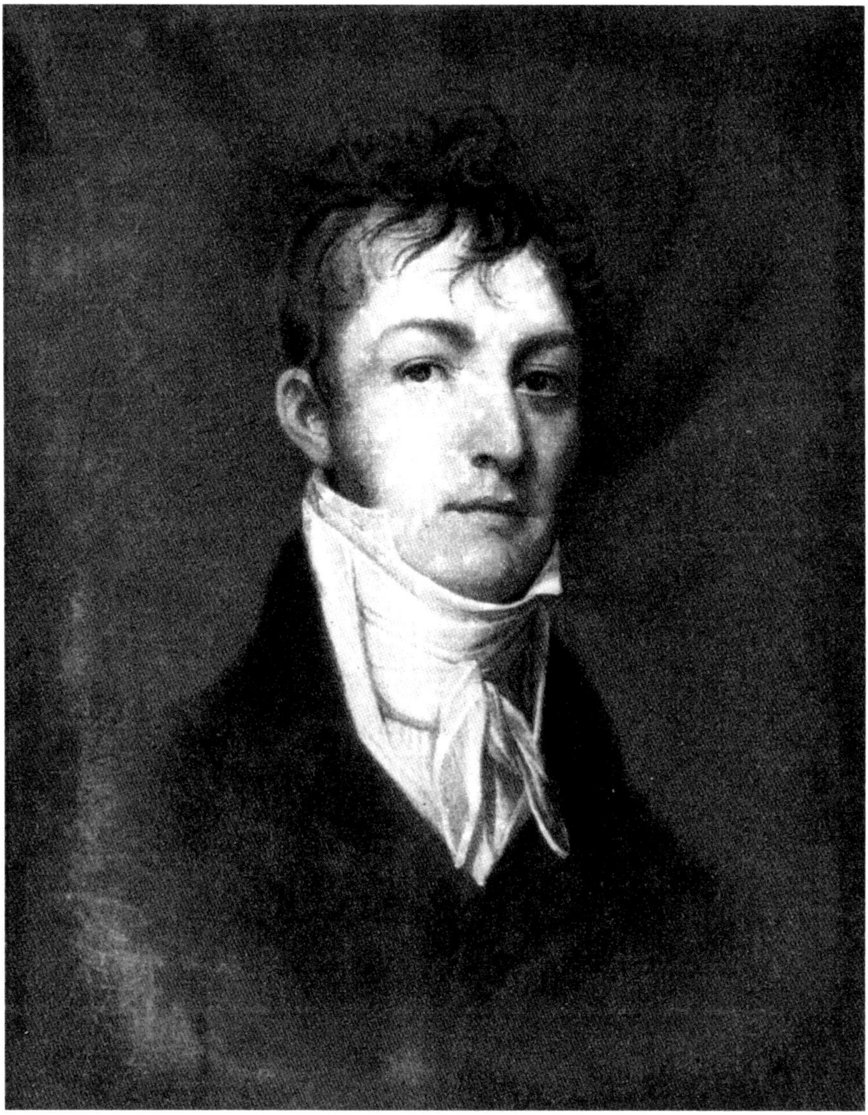

John Harrison (1773–1833), America's first industrial chemist. Priestly Lodge, his country home, was on the west side of Frankford Road, above Palmer.

Besides the family being known for the famous preacher, Sarah Richards, Thomas Harrison himself was known as an advocate of the abolition of slavery. His sixth son with Sarah Richards was John Harrison, reportedly America's first industrial chemist.

John Harrison was born in Philadelphia on December 17, 1773. He apprenticed at an early age to the chemist Townsend Speakman. Later, Harrison studied for two years in Europe, and for a time he studied under the famous Joseph Priestley, Unitarian minister, scientist and discoverer of oxygen. Harrison himself became a noted manufacturing chemist and the first to produce sulfuric acid in America. This led to him being called America's first industrial chemist. Sulfuric acid, or what used to be called "oil of vitriol," is a strong mineral acid and has many applications, including many chemical reactions and production processes. It is the most widely used chemical. Today, its uses include fertilizer manufacturing, ore processing, chemical synthesis, wastewater processing and oil refining.

Harrison married Lydia Leib, daughter of John George Leib and his wife Dorothy. The Leibs were well known in Philadelphia, being active in the government of the city and county. John and Lydia Harrison's son, George Leib Harrison, born October 28, 1811, would later take over his father's chemical business. George Leib Harrison later was invited to become a member of the firm of Powers and Weightman, which then became Powers, Weightman and Harrison, a well-known chemical establishment.

Besides his successful chemical business, John Harrison was captain of the Sixth Company in the Third Battalion of Philadelphia Militia. He also belonged to the "Fish House," and was elected a member of that "celebrated Schuylkill Fishing Company of the State in Schuylkill" in 1796. Harrison also took an active interest in the Franklin Institute, being a member of the first board of managers.

Harrison lived for many years at Priestley Lodge, named to honor his old friend and former teacher. The house was located on a small estate in Kensington on the west side of Frankford Road, above Palmer, where the old Kensington Depot was located, or more recently, the big empty lot near Septa's Berks Street EL stop, where they have plans to build the new art school for Kensington High School.

There is a painting of Priestley Lodge by the watercolorist William Kennedy, done when the house was still standing. It shows the building sitting off and away from the "road to Frankford." One of Harrison's "lead chambers," where he made his chemicals, was supposed to have been on his property in Kensington. An earlier chamber was in the Northern Liberties area.

Harrison died in 1833. The John Harrison Laboratory of Chemistry at the University of Pennsylvania was erected as a memorial to him by his grandsons, Charles Custis Harrison, Alfred Craven Harrison and William Welsh Harrison. There is a life-size sculpture of Harrison on the university campus.

WILLIAM CRAMP

FOUNDER OF WILLIAM CRAMP AND SONS SHIPYARD

Probably one of the more famous individuals to ever come out of Kensington was William Cramp. In Cramp's lifetime, he was world-renowned as one of the great shipbuilders of his time, if not in history. He was born September 22, 1807, on Otis Street, now Susquehanna, in what was then called East Kensington but is now Fishtown. The family name was originally Krampf, until the American Revolution, when, according to the fashion at that time, it was anglicized and became Cramp. The Krampfs came from southwestern Germany and were some of the first settlers in Kensington in the eighteenth century.

Cramp's family was one of a number of eighteenth-century German families who settled in Kensington and made their living through fishing. According to local historian Rich Remer, the families of Rice (Reiss), Baker (Backer), Beideman (Beidemann), Collar (Kohler), Gosser, Hill (Huhl), Hoffman, Mood (Mude), Pote (Poth) and Shibe were all German immigrants who started out as fishermen. Starting a fishing business was inexpensive and an easy step-up for early German immigrants. These German fishermen would eventually prosper well beyond anyone's belief, and they went on to control all the fishing rights on both sides of the Delaware River from Trenton to Cape May. These families put the "Fish" in "Fishtown."

Fishtown was that area of Kensington north of Palmer Street to the old Gunner's Run, sandwiched between Girard Avenue and the Delaware River. For most of Cramp's life he lived in Fishtown, on Vienna (Berks) above Queen (Richmond), Queen (Richmond) below Wood (Susquehanna), the rear of Palmer above Queen (Richmond), then at 65 Palmer and finally at 1033 and 1120 Palmer Street. When he was in the last years of his life, he finally moved out of the neighborhood and lived in the nineteenth-century "new money" neighborhood on 15th Street, near Master. This was

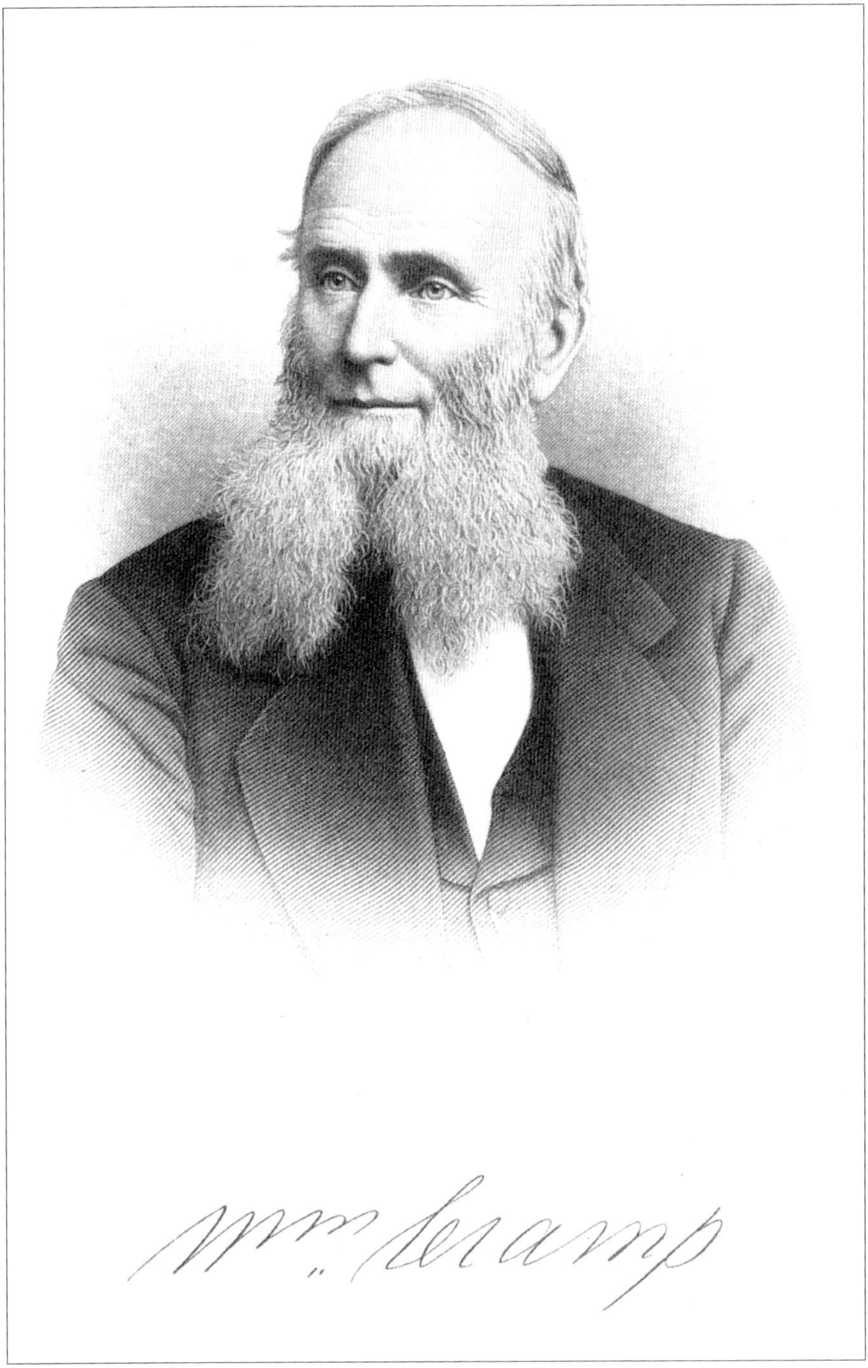

William Cramp (1807–1879), founder of the greatest shipyard in American history, spent most of his life living on Fishtown's Palmer Street.

a neighborhood to which many Kensingtonians who made their money in the later parts of the nineteenth century moved to live in fine townhouses or brownstone mansions.

After attending the public schools in Kensington, Cramp went to work in 1823 under Samuel Grice, a local Kensington shipbuilder. From Grice, Cramp learned his trade.

It was through marriage that William Cramp entered the shipbuilding business. He had married into a well-known family of shipbuilders. His wife was Sophia Miller, the daughter of Henry Miller, an early Kensington shipwright who, at twenty-one years old, "invested his small fortune in an interest in the cargo of a vessel in one of the earliest voyages after the Revolution from the port of Philadelphia to the East, taking in China, the Indies, and the Philippines." Cramp's mother-in-law was Elizabeth Byerly (or Birely), the sister of Kensington shipbuilder John Byerly, and one of Sophia's aunts was married to William Sutton, another noted shipbuilder of the day. Another of Cramp's wife's aunts was married to the shipbuilder John Bennett, who worked with his sons at Hoboken as shipwright and shipbuilder for the well-known Stevens family.

In 1830, after seven years with Grice, William Cramp opened his own shipyard at the foot of Susquehanna Street on the Delaware River. From this small beginning, his shipyard grew into the William Cramp and Sons Ship and Engine Building Company, once the most famous and largest private shipyard in the United States, known the world over. He constructed wood, ironclad, iron and, eventually, steel ships.

William Cramp and his wife had eleven children. In 1857 he took on two of his sons as partners (Charles H. and William M.), and then in 1863, he took on three more sons (Samuel H., Jacob C. and Theodore). Cramp remained president of the firm for almost fifty years, from its founding in 1830 until his death in Atlantic City on July 6, 1879. He had been in declining health since about 1877. He is buried at Laurel Hill Cemetery.

Cramp was a longtime member of the First Presbyterian Church of Kensington, where he was a trustee for over twenty years and donated one of the stained-glass windows. He initially started to study for the ministry under its pastor, the Reverend George Chandler, but due to poor health it was recommended that he take up an outdoor occupation. This was when he decided to go into the shipbuilding trade. In his lifetime he is said to have built 225 ships.

One can only imagine what type of preacher Cramp would have been, since his "second love," that of shipbuilding, resulted in one of the most famous shipyards in the history of the world.

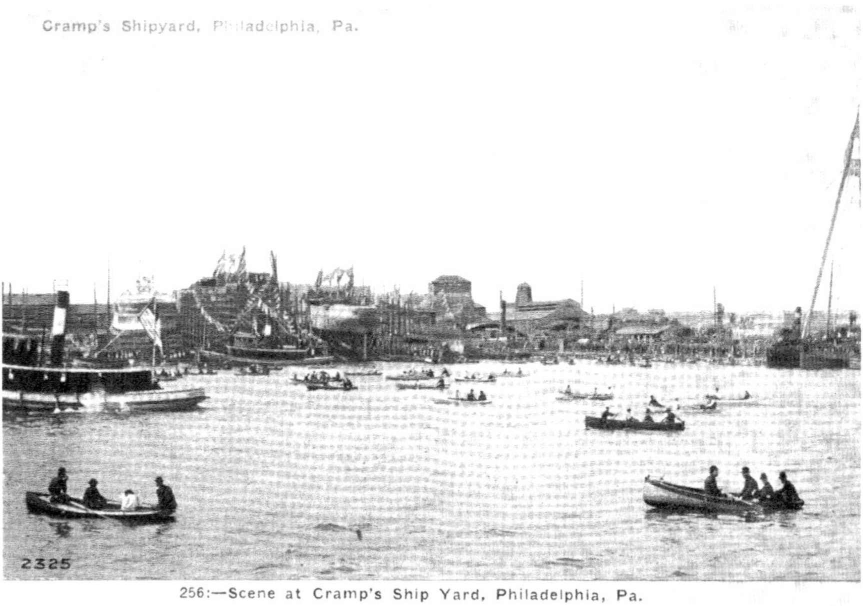

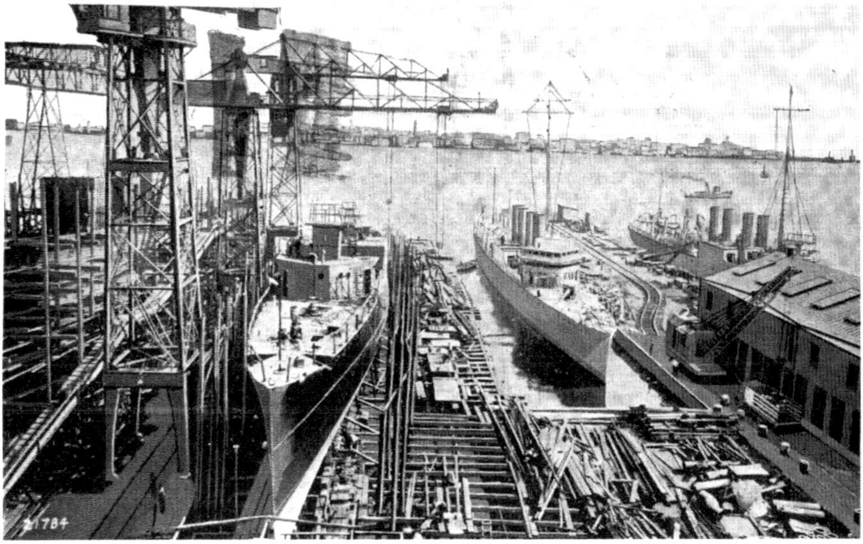

Postcards of William Cramp and Sons, circa 1900–1910. America's largest shipyard at one time, it was also a popular tourist attraction.

KENSINGTON'S SIXTH WARD

TEXTILE CAPITAL OF PHILADELPHIA

Between the years 1820 and 1854, Kensington was a self-governing district. In 1854, all of Philadelphia County was consolidated with the city of Philadelphia, and Kensington became one of the neighborhoods of the enlarged city. In 1850, the District of Kensington was divided into eight wards. One particular ward stood out as the heart of the textile industry for all of Philadelphia—the old Sixth Ward. Professor Philip Scranton, in his book *Proprietary Capitalism* (Cambridge University Press, 1983), takes a detailed look at the history of this famous textile area.

Kensington first became self-governing in March of 1820. Fourteen years later, in April of 1834, the population had grown so much that it was found necessary, for governing purposes, to divide the district up into five separate wards. In February 1846, the ward boundaries of Kensington were again redrawn, this time adding a Sixth and Seventh Ward.

The population had increased so much during the past decade (1836–1846) that the Sixth Ward was created out of the old Third Ward. The new Sixth Ward was located between Frankford Avenue and 3rd Street, and from Girard Avenue north to Oxford Street, and the old Third Ward shifted to the west of 3rd Street.

The Sixth Ward was the area that saw some of the heaviest rioting during the anti–Irish Catholic riots of May 1844, a time when Protestants from Fishtown, the Northern Liberties and Southwark attacked the newly arrived Irish Catholic immigrants. The increase in population that had taken place was mainly Irish Catholics who became associated with Saint Michael's Church at 2nd and Jefferson Streets. Many of them were hand weavers, drawn to Kensington for work in the textile industry.

Scranton states:

> *Three-quarters of the textile firms and workers were counted in the central and adjacent Third and Sixth wards. With 1,600 workers and forty-nine firms, the Sixth Ward was the most heavily packed textile neighborhood in Kensington in 1850.*

He linked the manufacturing census of 1850 with the population census of the same year, coming up with some interesting insights. Of the forty-nine firms he identified in the Sixth Ward, he linked forty-five of them to the population census. He found that forty-four of the owners of these firms either lived close to, or at, the worksite in Kensington's Sixth Ward. Of the forty-five manufacturers that Scranton linked, thirty-three of them were Irish born. The Irish master weavers tended to run their handlooms "on cottons, mixed goods, and carpets."

Other information he gathered showed an "aging cotton handloom group with younger shop masters taking up carpet manufacture, a hand trade that showed a long-term rise" from the 1840s to 1870s.

By reviewing the 1850 population census, Scranton found that the "bulk of the Irish textile employers in 1850 Kensington were present to welcome the famine-era immigrants to their workshops, rather than being new arrivals themselves." And welcome them they did, as famine-era immigrants filled many Kensington blocks.

Scranton also found that handloom proprietors only had to rent a workshop or build a shed for their looms—a fraction of the cost of the larger, power-loom factories. The average investment was only $90 per worker, as compared to $555 per worker at the large power-loom works in Manayunk or Old City.

The hand weavers generally owned their own looms, and since hand weaving was a skilled job, they could, on average, earn about $216 per year (women about $72 per year). In today's money that would amount to approximately $41,000 for a man, $14,000 for a woman.

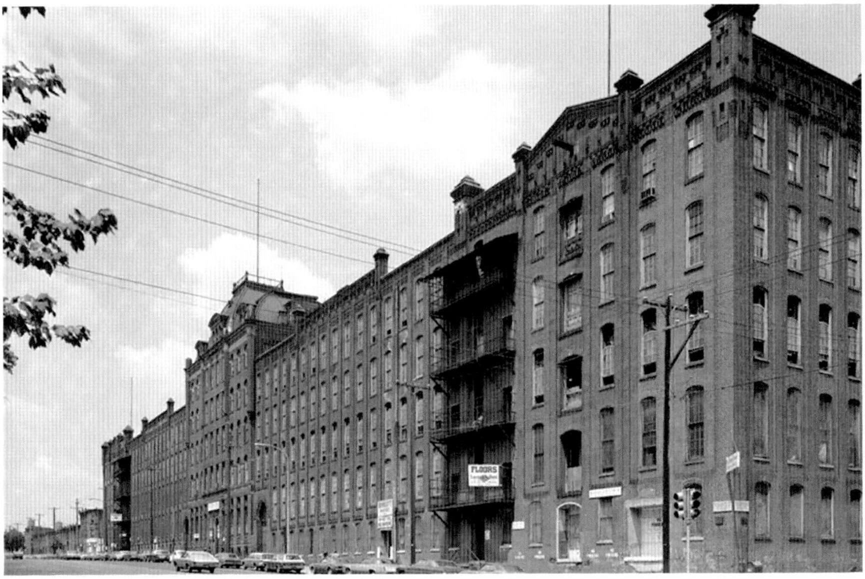

John Bromley and Sons, 201–263 East Lehigh Avenue, is now the site of a welfare office. *Courtesy of the Library of Congress, Prints and Photographs Division.*

Since the handloom proprietors found it difficult to upgrade to the power-loom factory level (their profits at handloom production were not great enough for the investment needed), many of the masters instead invested in real estate, often providing housing for their workers, or even boarding them.

An old, small-frame house in Kensington could be purchased for $150 ($28,500 today), an old brick house was about $300 ($57,200 today) and a brand-new, six-room house was about $1,000 ($190,000 today). With a hand weaver earning about $216 a year, they were not in a position to purchase a new home, so they would have to either rent a home or buy an old wood frame, which would have been affordable. A decent house could be rented for $50 to $60 per year, so even if a hand weaver made the equivalent of $41,000 today, his rent would be equivalent to almost $800 a month.

These little tidbits give some insight into a long gone way of life. The old Sixth Ward remained a leader in Kensington's textile business sector for a little while longer, until the Norris estate began to be broken up in the late 1840s. At that time, a number of firms, including the great mills of the Bromley family, started moving north, and the areas around Front and York, Front and Lehigh and along Allegheny Avenue became the new focal points for the textile industry in Kensington.

EDWIN HENRY FITLER

KENSINGTON-BORN MAYOR OF PHILADELPHIA

When Edwin Henry Fitler (1825–1896) was laid to rest at Laurel Hill Cemetery, the honorary pallbearers included the governor of Pennsylvania, the mayor of Philadelphia, an ex-mayor of Philadelphia, the provost of the University of Pennsylvania and some of the leading businessmen of Philadelphia. Mourners were plentiful and had the names of Elkins, Widener, Biddle and Singerly, names famous in Philadelphia's history. Who was Edwin H. Fitler? And why was this Kensingtonian so respected?

You may have heard of the Center City neighborhood of Fitler Square, but what do you know about the man for whom it is named? Edwin H. Fitler was the son of a leather merchant who lived at 2nd and Otter (Wildey)

Streets, in the old District of Kensington. In 1846, after studying law briefly, Fitler entered the cordage factory of George J. Weaver, at Germantown Avenue and 10th Street. In two years' time he became so knowledgeable that he was invited into the business as a full partner. The firm changed its name to George J. Weaver and Company. An 1857 advertisement had this to say about Fitler's establishment:

> *Messrs. Weaver, Fitler & Co. are proprietors of the Fairhill Steam Cordage Works, manufacturing every style of Manilla, Tarred and Italian Ropes, Tow Lines for canal boats, all the various styles of Carpet and seine Twine, &c. This is the largest manufacturing establishment in this business in Philadelphia. They do an exclusive wholesale business, and merchants throughout the country can find no better establishment to order and make purchases from than Weaver, Fitler & Co.,…*They *Have constantly on hand, a full assortment of Ropes, &c; Anchors and Chains of all Sizes; American, Italian and Russian Hemp Ropes of any size or description Made to order on short notice.*

In 1859, Fitler bought out Weaver and changed the company's name to Edwin H. Fitler and Company. Eventually Fitler's two sons (Edwin and William) would enter the business. The offices of the company were located downtown on Water Street, on the Delaware River waterfront, near their wharf. About 1880, the old works at 10th and Germantown Streets was seen as inadequate and a new works was built in Bridesburg.

Fitler eventually moved to the 1600 block of Walnut Street, only a short walk from the Manufacturer's Club, where he became active and served for a time as the vice-president. He was also elected president of the American Cordage Manufacturers' Association. During the Civil War, Fitler organized and equipped a company of men from his cordage works. He was also an early member of the Union League and onetime president of that organization. He served in many other capacities on various philanthropic institutions' boards.

In 1876, Fitler was a Republican presidential elector for Pennsylvania. His abilities in business and finance were so great that he was sought out as the Republican choice for mayor of Philadelphia in 1887. He won by thirty thousand votes. As the first mayor under the new city charter, Fitler's duties were immense. According to his obituary in a local Philadelphia newspaper:

> *The whole city administration needed to be organized, competent heads of departments appointed, and methods of action devised for which there was no precedent in the history of the city. He fulfilled these duties to the*

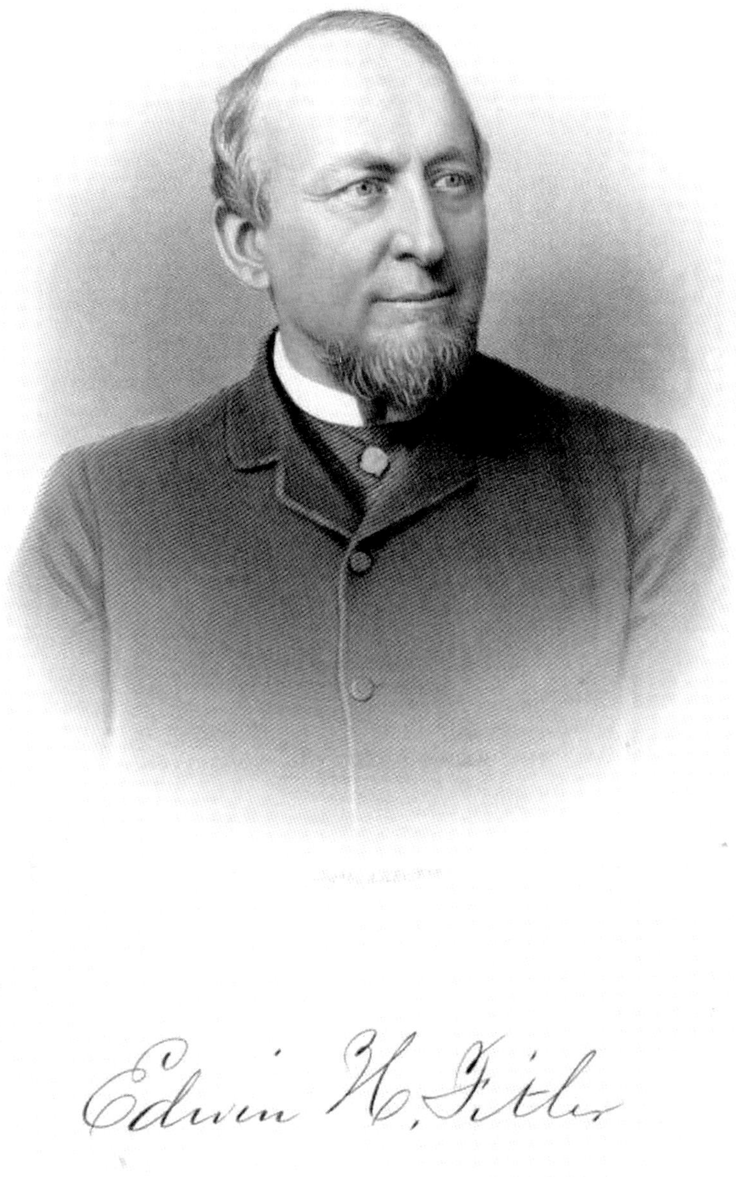

Edwin H. Fitler (1825–1896) was nominated by Pennsylvanians as candidate for president of the United States. He grew up near 2nd and George Streets.

> *general satisfaction of the public and left a thoroughly organized system of municipal government to his successors.*

He was so well respected that his name was presented at Chicago in 1888 by Philadelphia delegates as their choice for president of the United States. While he did not seek the office, he did appreciate the honor of the mere mention of his name in that capacity.

Though Fitler moved up and out of Kensington, he never forgot his roots. He remained a supporter of the Kensington Soup Society.

During the rise of Fitler's career, he also took in another Kensingtonian to help run the business. Conrad F. Clothier (1829–1886) was associated with the First Presbyterian Church of Kensington, a church in which one of the stained-glass windows is dedicated to him. He became the bookkeeper for Fitler's company. When Edwin H. Fitler bought out his partner George J. Weaver and took over the company, he invited Clothier to become a partner in the new firm that was created. In 1854, the year before joining the Weaver and Fitler firm, Clothier married Mary Victoria Byerly, a member of a well-known local Kensington shipbuilding family who was also related to the famed shipbuilder William Cramp.

Edwin H. Fitler died on May 31, 1896, and was buried at Laurel Hill Cemetery. He was a local Kensington boy who became one of Philadelphia's richest citizens, its mayor and its choice for president of the United States. Fitler's granddaughter was Happy Rockefeller, the second wife of Vice-President Nelson A. Rockefeller.

Hamilton Disston

Industrialist and Real Estate Tycoon

It would be great to own land in Florida—a house with a quarter of an acre. How about owning 5.5 million acres in Florida? Sounds crazy right? But this was a reality for a fellow who spent a good part of his life growing up in Kensington. The fellow's name was Hamilton Disston, the son of famed saw manufacturer Henry Disston.

Henry Disston immigrated to Philadelphia when he was fourteen years old. His father died after only three days in America. Henry stayed in

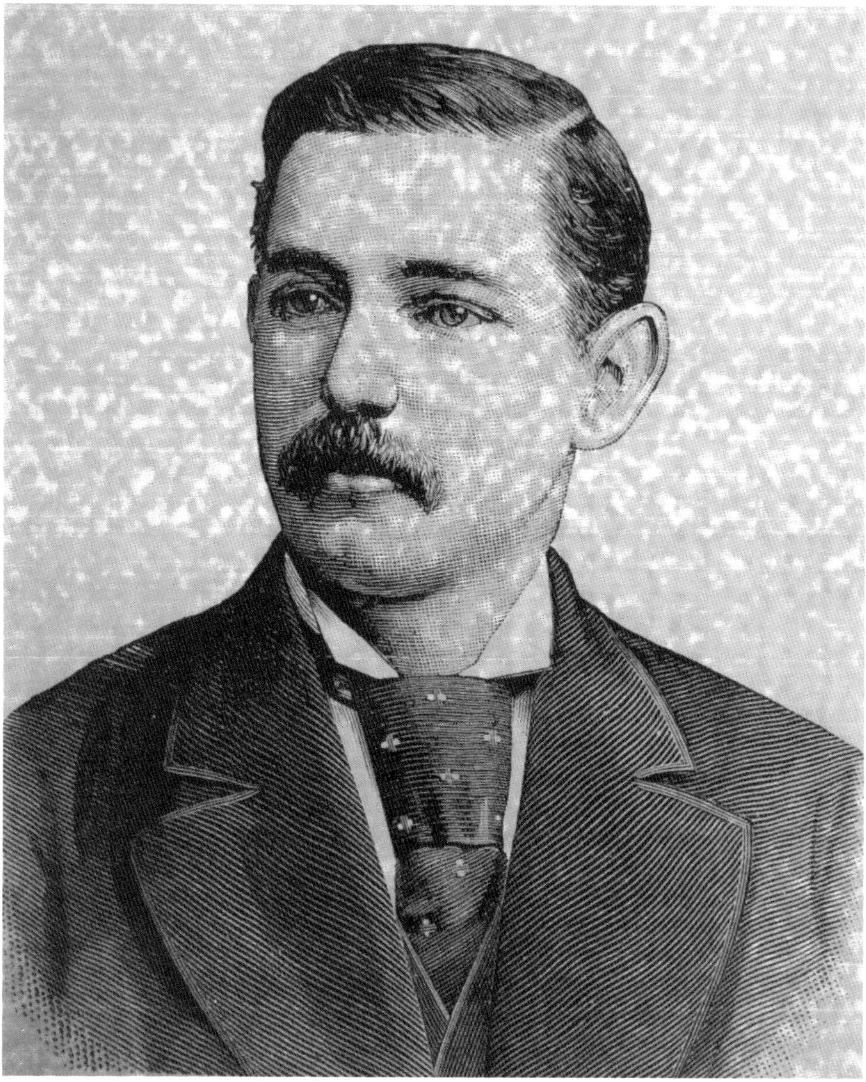

Hamilton Disston, son of the founder of Disston and Sons' Saw Works, grew up at Front and Laurel Streets. He later owned 15 percent of Florida.

Philadelphia and took a job with a local saw manufacturer. In 1840, after about six years of working, he had acquired enough skills and money to venture out on his own.

Despite initial setbacks he became successful. In the mid-1840s, he purchased a lot at Front and Laurel Streets in Kensington. It was here that he built his saw works. It was at about this time that Hamilton Disston was born.

By 1850, Disston's saws began to be considered superior to those of his competitors. The Civil War brought a boost to his business. His Laurel Street plant eventually covered eight acres.

By 1871, Henry decided that the area around Front and Laurel Streets had become too congested, making it difficult to expand, so he purchased land in the Tacony section of Philadelphia on the Delaware River. He eventually purchased close to four hundred acres, leaving forty acres for his business and the rest for the development of a community for his workers. This was how the Tacony neighborhood developed.

Disston's saw works became famous the world over.

Henry died in 1878, and his son Hamilton took over the business. Hamilton started as an apprentice at the saw works in 1859. The business began moving to Tacony in the 1870s, but the Front and Laurel Street plant did not close down until 1899.

During those early years, from the mid-1840s through the 1860s, Hamilton and his parents lived in Kensington, near the saw works. But by 1870, Hamilton, like his father, moved to the "new money" neighborhood of North Broad Street, where many Kensington manufacturers relocated after acquiring wealth.

Besides being a mover and a shaker in Republican politics during the 1870s and 1880s, Hamilton also served for a time as Philadelphia fire commissioner, as well as the first Fairmount Park commissioner. His interest in real estate led him to go into business in Florida. He had a contract with the State of Florida to drain land and reclaim it. The reclaimed land would be split between Hamilton's company and the state.

In 1881, with Florida in debt due to the Civil War, Hamilton purchased an additional 4 million acres of Florida, which helped to bail out the state from its debt. He later added over 1.5 million acres of land, giving him over 5.5 million acres, or over 15 percent ownership of the state of Florida. He was the largest landowner in America in his day and the main motivator for the development of Florida. Not bad for a kid who spent his formative years at Front and Laurel.

Besides his land company, Hamilton also developed railroads, bought a half interest in a large sugar plantation and ran a steamboat company.

The early 1890s were the beginning of the financial end for Hamilton. Besides the economy tanking in 1893, a bounty on sugar production was taken away by President Cleveland the next year, and on top of that, freezes in the winters of 1893 and 1894 wiped out much of the income from some of his projects. Land prices also started to drop. Expansion of the railroad into Florida made his steamboat company useless and drew people away from the areas he was developing.

The banks were about to foreclose on Hamilton for a $1,000,000 loan; however, he beat them to the punch and dropped dead at the age of forty-eight. Mystery surrounds his death. One paper reported that he committed suicide, putting a bullet in his head while sitting in the bathtub of his North Broad Street home. This was confirmed by a cousin. However, many papers across the country reported that he died from a heart attack. The coroner's report stated that the death was from natural causes. Could it have been a coverup by the family to avoid public embarrassment?

Some thought Hamilton was distraught over economic ruin and feared that his personal ruin might affect the family business, as the business had been used to get the $1,000,000 loan. After Hamilton's death, the family was able to pull together resources to pay off the debt and the old saw works was not affected.

So ends the great and sad story of a kid who grew up in Kensington.

PART III

RECREATION IN THE NEIGHBORHOOD

BACHELOR'S HALL

KENSINGTON'S FIRST GENTLEMEN'S CLUB

When Anthony Palmer took up residence in the old Fairman Mansion (at what would be today's Penn Treaty Park) about the year 1729–30, he began laying out the current grid of streets and advertising the lots for his town of Kensington. It was easy for him to find buyers because property in Philadelphia had become expensive and waterfront lots were hard to come by. A number of these first purchasers in Kensington were fishermen or shipwrights, and according to historian Rich Remer, "the mariners, watermen, and especially fishermen tended to live higher up river in the triangle formed by Montgomery and Aramingo Avenues and both sides of Richmond Street to the river," while the shipwrights tended to live in "the southwest area of Kensington, along Shackamaxon and Marlborough Streets," in the neighborhood close to where Bachelor's Hall stood.

Bachelor's Hall was "a private banqueting clubhouse run by Isaac Norris and his colleagues," and when first built, there was no Kensington to encroach on it. The great annalist of Philadelphia, John Fanning Watson, states that Bachelor's Hall was once a celebrated place of "gluttony and good living, but highly genteel and select." According to Watson, Bachelor's Hall was "situated in Kensington on the main river street, a little above the present market house." When Watson was writing in 1830, the "present market house" was the old Beach Street Market, situated near the foot of Frankford Avenue and Beach Street, with Beach being the "main river street."

Bachelor's Hall was said to be a "square building of considerable beauty, with pilasters." The club was built for a select group of city gentlemen, including Robert Charles, William Masters, John Sober, P. Graeme and Isaac Norris. The last survivor of the club was to take possession of the premises. Norris was the one who wound up taking over the hall.

Watson states that the hall had a fine open view to the scenery on the Delaware and that "tea parties were made there frequently for the ladies of their acquaintance." Bachelor's Hall was once lent (around 1770–71) to John Murray, the Universalist preacher, "keeping then the doctrine cannon shot distance from the city."

The reference here is that Universalism was not yet dear to the hearts of Quaker Philadelphia, nor was a bachelor's hall very much liked. Thus it was located in what would have been, back then, the "suburbs."

Watson says that while the place was in vogue, it received the flattery of the muses. One particularly famous poem written about Bachelor's Hall was by George Webb, a colleague of Benjamin Franklin and a member of his "Junto" club:

Fired with the business of the noisy town,
The weary Batchelors their cares disown;
For this loved seat they all at once prepare,
And long to breathe the sweets of country air;
On nobler thoughts their active minds employ,
And a select variety enjoy.
'Tis not a revel, or lascivious night,
That to this hall the Batchelors invite;
Much less shall impious doctrines here be taught,
Blush ye accusers at the very thought:
For other, O, far other ends designed,
To mend the heart, and cultivate the mind.

While Webb may have been trying to convince the readers that Bachelor's Hall was just a place for fellows to get together and discuss the latest books or ideas, many in Philadelphia thought it was a den of iniquity. Watson, in his *Annals of Philadelphia*, states:

> *The mysteries of the place, however, were all unknown to the vulgar, and for that very reason they gave loose to many conjectures, which finally passed for current tales, as a bachelor's place, where maidens were inveigled and deceived. I had myself heard stories of it when a boy, which thrilled my soul with horror, without one word of truth for its foundation.*

Watson tells us that during the year 1777, the British were burning most of the outlying mansions and buildings as part of their fortification of the northern border of the city of Philadelphia. At that time, the city's northern boundary was Vine Street, and a number of Americans were sniping from various buildings as the British patrolled the area. Francis Hopkinson's "Old Bachelor" has some verses on the burning of Bachelor's Hall.

In its early years, about the year 1729, Bachelor's Hall was said to have had the first botanical garden, used for the "cultivation of plants having medicinal properties." It was described as being near Allen and Shackamaxon Streets. More accurately, Bachelor's Hall was located at about Shackamaxon and Hall Streets, with Hall Street being present-day Beach Street.

POINT PLEASANT

A COLONIAL RESORT

It might be difficult to picture, but the area at Popular Street and the Delaware River, where the Waterfront Square towers are now being built, was once known as Point Pleasant. The peninsula-like piece of land lying between the old Cohocksink Creek (Canal Street) and the Delaware River was at one time a resort, surrounded on three sides by water—one side a creek, the other a bay of sorts and the third the Delaware River. The area had an inn, a tavern and opportunities for sport shooting nearby.

In his *Annals of Philadelphia* (1830), John Watson tells us that the Delaware River formerly made a great inroad upon the land at the mouth of the Cohocksink Creek, "making there a large and shallow bay, extending from Point Pleasant down to Warder's long wharf, near Green Street," and that back in the 1790s, the water used to come up daily to the houses at Front and Coates (Fairmount) Streets. The area of the bay (which at that time excluded the present streets east of Front Street) was "an immense plane of spatterdocks, a common North American water lily, which filled the bay from the end of Warder's wharf at Green Street and on a line with Point Pleasant."

Watson also mentions:

> *The lower end of Coates' Street was then lower than now; and in freshets the river laid across Front Street. All the ten or twelve houses north of Coates' Street, on the east side, were built on made ground, and their little yards were supported with wharf logs, and bush willows as trees. At the then mouth of* the *Cohocksink was a wooden drawbridge, then the only communication to Kensington, which crossed at Leib's house opposite to Poplar Lane; from thence a raised causeway ran across to Point Pleasant. The stone bridge north of it at Front Street leading to Kensington was not then in existence. On the outside of this causeway the river covered, and spatterdocks grew, and on the inside there was a great extent of marshy ground alternately wet and dry, with the ebbing and flowing of the tide; the creek was embanked on the east side. The marsh was probably two hundred feet wide where the causeway at the stone bridge now runs…The marsh grounds of Cohocksink used to afford good shooting for woodcock and snipe, &c.*

One early advertisement for Point Pleasant by William Masters, on August 1, 1765, stated that on the last day of that month, Masters would be selling a large, three-story brick house on Germantown Road, at the upper end of 2nd

Street, and if a person were interested, he could contact Masters at his distillery at "Point Pleasant, near Kensington." Masters owned a fairly large amount of land in the area that stretched north and west to Girard Avenue and beyond.

On May 24, 1770, another business advertisement for Point Pleasant appeared, printed in the *Pennsylvania Gazette*, for Elizabeth Phillips's cured sturgeon. Her business was advertised as being located next to William Masters's distillery, and this ad appears to be one of the earliest mentions of a woman selling fish in the area.

Phillips was again advertising her kegs of cured sturgeon, done in the "Baltick manner," in the *Pennsylvania Gazette* on April 30, 1772. There was also a 1771 advertisement for "an assortment of ironmongery and sundry other articles" at the house of Thomas Savadge, at Point Pleasant, in the Northern Liberties of the city of Philadelphia, near Kensington.

By 1820, a fire company was founded at Point Pleasant, called, appropriately enough, the "Point Pleasant Fire Company." It was founded in July of 1820 and was located on the Delaware River at the mouth of the Cohocksink Creek.

Because the embankment of the creek elevated Point Pleasant somewhat, the British forces at the time of the American Revolution built a battery and fort at this location on the riverbank, just above Laurel Street. It helped the British to defend Philadelphia from the Americans who might try coming from the north down the Delaware River, or along Frankford and Germantown Roads or the Point Road (Richmond Street). The Brits also dammed the Cohocksink Creek, flooding the marshes even more and helping their defenses on the northern end of the city. It wasn't until after the Revolution that the area started to be developed fully.

With all of the development going on in this area of Kensington today, it looks like it will soon again be a resort of sorts. And who says history doesn't repeat itself?

BATHTOWN

KENSINGTON'S COLONIAL SPA

If you take a stroll down "Liberties' Walk," the short, two-block, mixed-use shopping center between 2nd and Bodine Streets and between George and Wildey Streets, you certainly won't have the impression that at one time you could have vacationed there, taking hot baths and relaxing away from the hustle and bustle of Philadelphia.

From an advertisement in the *Pennsylvania Gazette*, dated August 22, 1765, we learn the following:

> *Town of BATH in the Northern Liberties in the City of Philadelphia. JOHN WHITE, living in the NEW BATH, humbly proposes, by the Assistance of his Wife, to Accomodate Ladies and Gentlemen with Breakfasting, on the best Tea, Coffee, and Chocolate, with plenty of GOOD CREAM, &c., which articles may also be had in an Afternoon. He likewise hopes to give Satisfaction to any Persons whose Health may require their going to the Bath, by his attendance and by furnishing them with Brushes and proper Towels; and as Order and Decency is naturally required in such an Undertaking, he further hopes to approve himself capable of conducting and salutary Purposes, which the Founder originally intended, and now hopes to see effected. He takes the Liberty and subscribes himself the Publick's most obedient humble Servant. JOHN WHITE.*
>
> *N.B. The Bath being now opened, Tickets for the Bathing Season may be had of him.*

In Joseph Jackson's *Encyclopedia of Philadelphia*, the information on Bathtown is rather scarce, but he did pinpoint the area:

> *Established in the year 1765…situated near the Germantown Road, between the Cohocksink Creek and the Globe Mill…The western boundary of Bath Town was between Pitt Street (afterward called St. John Street) and Third Street.*

Jackson's Pitt Street, afterward called Saint John Street, is present-day American Street. The Cohocksink was long ago made into a culvert, and starting from the Delaware River, it runs under the present-day streets of Canal, Allen, Hancock, Laurel, Bodine and Cambridge.

Earlier, in 1830, that great Philadelphia annalist John Fanning Watson had this to say about Bathtown:

> *Bath town, in the Northern Liberties* was *brought into much celebrity by the influence of Dr. Kearsley…Their house at that day stood on a pleasant farm, called White's farm, having about the house a grove of grateful shade—itself on a green bank gently declining into the Cohocksinc creek. The house was sometimes called the "Rose of Bath," because of the sign of a rose attached to*

> *the house. The house is now standing, dismantled of all its former rural and attractive charms, a two story building, on the next lot north of the Methodist church in St. John Street; and the spring, now obliterated, once flowed on the south side of that church, on ground now converted into a tanyard by Pritchet, nearly due east from the Third street stone bridge. The spring, over which Dr. Kearsley had erected a bath house, stood about twenty to twenty-five feet west from the line of St. John street, on the southern side of the tanyard, as I have been told. I mention the location with such particularity, that it may at some day cause a better speculation for some of our citizens, to revive it there by digging or boring, than that of "Jacob's Well" at New York. "The town of Bath," so imposing a name, never existed but on charts. It was a speculation once to make a town there, but it did not take.*

Dr. John Kearsley (1684–1772), the founder of Bathtown, discovered early on that the spring in the area was good for medicinal purposes. Kearsley was also the fellow that designed Christ Church (2nd and Market Streets) and the statehouse (Independence Hall). He served for many years in the Pennsylvania General Assembly.

Although Watson states that Bathtown was located in the Northern Liberties, he is talking about the township, not the district, as the district only became incorporated in 1803. Bathtown sat on the north side of the Cohocksink Creek, thus in the boundaries of the historical District of Kensington.

Roughly speaking, Bathtown sat along both sides of 2nd Street, from at least 180 feet east of 2nd Street all the way west to American Street, with the Cohocksink Creek as the southern border and the northern border near Germantown Avenue. Visitors could have arrived at Bathtown via the road to Germantown, the Cohocksink Creek or 2nd Street.

Today, the old Bathtown area is being revived. I haven't seen anyone hanging up the "Rose of Bath" sign yet, but who knows, maybe this column will inspire someone to put in some hot baths again?

Fishtown Park

The Kensington Water Works was once located on the Delaware River at the Otis Street (Susquehanna Avenue) wharf. Some years after Philadelphia County was consolidated into the city of Philadelphia (1854), the new city government closed the Kensington Water Works because of the polluted nature of the water it drew from. However, the wharf itself remained in the city's possession for a number of years thereafter. This wharf was the original Cramp Shipyard, acquired by William Cramp from his mother Catherine Rice, who inherited it from her family's estate.

While the wharf went two hundred feet out into the Delaware River, the waterworks' suction pipes sat just below the mouth of the polluted creek, Gunner's Run (now under Aramingo Avenue). By late 1861, with complaints about the quality of the water and outbreaks of typhoid fever, the Kensington Water Works was called a nuisance and cries erupted to rid the city of it. The waterworks was soon shut down and no longer pumped water from the Delaware. The Kensington reservoir at 6th and Lehigh Streets was soon refilled with water drawn from the Schuylkill.

The Kensington Water Works took up only part of the Otis Street wharf, with the rest of the wharf being a recreational pier. From an article in the *Philadelphia Inquirer* of 1881, we find that the pier was called "Fishtown Park" and predated Penn Treaty Park (1893) by at least forty-some-odd years, if not many more. As reported in the paper, it was a popular resort for residents of Kensington:

> *During the extremely hot evenings, particularly on Sunday evening, the long pier at Otis street wharf has been thronged with young and old people from the neighborhood in the immediate vicinity, to enjoy the breeze from the river. Last evening was no exception to the rule, and the "breathing spot" was crowded with all ages, from the old grandmother with her frilled cap and spectacles, to the baby in the coach, which by the way, were quite numerous. Loving swains, arm-in-arm with the object of their affections, were also largely represented. Peanut and lemonade venders plied their business, doing a lively trade.*
>
> *This wharf has always been a famous resort for people living in that section of the city. Some years ago two rows of trees, running out to the end of the pier, adorned the wharf and added to its attractiveness. However, the trees were destroyed by visitors who cut the trunks with their penknives. The trees were finally removed and replaced by a railing on both sides and two rows of benches. At the time when the trees were in good order the place was very much frequented, and was commonly known as Fishtown Park.*

The pier was also a stopping point for excursion boats during the last decades of the nineteenth century and into the twentieth century. One steamer, chartered by the Sanitarium for Sick Children, would pick up neighborhood children and parents for a ride on the river and then on to

Windmill Island. The island was located in the middle of the Delaware River, opposite Center City. At the island, children could get some fresh air and a wholesome lunch and enjoy a respite from the "atmosphere of dark courts and alleys." Eventually, in 1887, the sanitarium moved to New Jersey, to West Deptford's Red Bank section, and the trips were kept up well into the twentieth century, departing at that point from Penn Treaty Park. Fishtown's old-timers will remember these "Soupy Island" excursions. Even though Red Bank was not an "island," the early stories of Windmill Island were handed down, and the excursions to Red Bank were still known as "Soupy Island" to Fishtowners.

The waterworks wharf was also often a starting point, or turnaround point, for boat races, or regattas, on the Delaware River. The races would run from the waterworks or Tinicum and back; or from Chester to Gloucester, New Jersey, to the waterworks and back to Chester. The wharf was also the scene of William D. Moore's public exhibition of his aquatic velocipede in 1875, the aquatic counterpart to the success of the bicycle.

As with any popular water spot, there were reports of many drownings, or bodies being found floating at the waterworks wharf. This may have been a result of activity at the wharf, or perhaps the bodies were floating down from Gunner's Run. Since the Delaware River makes an abrupt turn at this point, an eddy was created, which caused objects to gather, including bodies.

The Anthony Atwood Sunday School first met in 1855 in the former Kensington Water Works building. Later, this Sunday school would evolve into the Siloam ME Church and move down the street to Susquehanna Avenue, above Thompson, until just a few years ago, when it closed its doors.

SHACKAMAXON SQUARE

It is hard to imagine today, but the small cement island at the northwest corner of Frankford and Delaware Avenues was once part of a larger park called Shackamaxon Square. According to Scharf and Westcott's *History of Philadelphia*, the history of this park has a curious beginning:

> *When the Point Pleasant Market, at the intersection of Frankford road and Maiden Street, was built, in 1819...*by the *commissioners of the district of Northern Liberties, there was left on its western side an open space, which it was proposed to convert into a public square. Upon the incorporation of the district of Kensington in 1820, authority over the market was vested in the Kensington commissioners, and...over the square. As the market was deserted by dealers, it was torn down, and the grounds were neglected until, in 1845, the commissioners resolved that two dozen seats should be placed in the square, and that it should be kept open, under the supervision of the police, from six o'clock in the morning to eight o'clock in the evening, daily, from the 1st of May to the 31st of August. At a later period in the same year an ordinance was passed for the regulation of the public square, prohibiting injury to the trees or benches, making it an offense for any one to lie down in the square, or to use insulting language to any person passing through the grounds. The commissioners gave no name to the place.*

By looking at the various "Digest of Acts of Assembly" for the District of Kensington, when it was self-governing (1820–1854), and by looking at old maps, one can piece together the history and boundaries of this park.

In 1851, Kensington's commissioners passed a law stating that the public square "bounded on the northwest by the Frankford road, on the southeast by Beach Street, on the southwest by Maiden Street, and on the northeast by Manderson Street, should be thereafter called Shackamaxon Square." Today we know Maiden Street by the name of Laurel Street, and Manderson Street is now that little right-turn lane onto Frankford Avenue when traveling south on Delaware Avenue. Beach Street still exists, but it is now east of Delaware Avenue, a reminder that the park was obliterated when this road came through.

In 1850, Kensington's commissioners ordered that the "clerk of the Beach Street Market be directed to take the public square at Maiden and Beach streets under his charge." The Beach Street Market (Point Pleasant Market) was located on the west side of Beach, from Shackamaxon Street to the "Bridge or Brown Street," and the "south side of Manderson Street from Frankford Road to Beach Street." The bridge would have been the one across the old Cohocksink Creek, Kensington's southern border.

When the market declined in the 1840s (perhaps because of the industrial buildup of the area and the emergence of other markets, most notably the nearby Franklin Market along Girard Avenue, east and west of Front Street), an emphasis was placed on refurbishing the adjacent public square area. According to Scharf and Westcott:

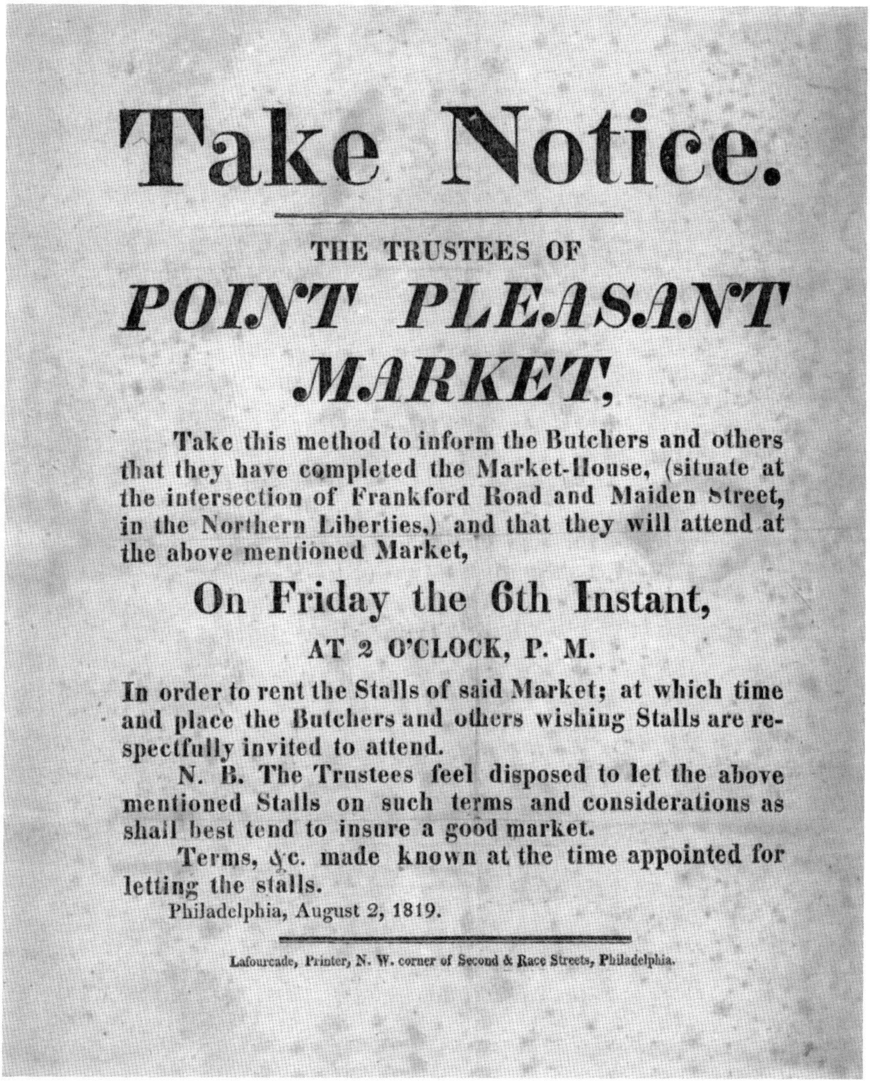

Take Notice.

THE TRUSTEES OF

POINT PLEASANT MARKET,

Take this method to inform the Butchers and others that they have completed the Market-House, (situate at the intersection of Frankford Road and Maiden Street, in the Northern Liberties,) and that they will attend at the above mentioned Market,

On Friday the 6th Instant,

AT 2 O'CLOCK, P. M.

In order to rent the Stalls of said Market; at which time and place the Butchers and others wishing Stalls are respectfully invited to attend.

N. B. The Trustees feel disposed to let the above mentioned Stalls on such terms and considerations as shall best tend to insure a good market.

Terms, &c. made known at the time appointed for letting the stalls.

Philadelphia, August 2, 1819.

Lafourcade, Printer, N. W. corner of Second & Race Streets, Philadelphia.

A Point Pleasant Market broadside. Philadelphia, 1819. *Courtesy of the Library of Congress, Printed Ephemera Collection.*

The commissioners were authorized to keep the inclosure in good order, for the purposes intended, and to tear down and remove the market-house fronting on Beach Street whenever they should deem it expedient to do so. This privilege was soon exercised, as the market-house had become useless, except as a resort for the disreputable classes of the vicinity.

In 1851, Kensington's commissioners stated that the square would be properly enclosed and planted with trees, and no buildings would be erected. With later maps showing a bathhouse located at the square (about 1876), it appears that once Kensington became part of the city, all bets were off.

It is hard to imagine Shackamaxon Square today. There is only a tiny triangular piece of cement left to this park, which is barren of trees and benches, but according to *Hopkins's Atlas* (circa 1875) the square measured 120 by 150 feet, with a center circular area and two wide paths crisscrossing at angles through the park.

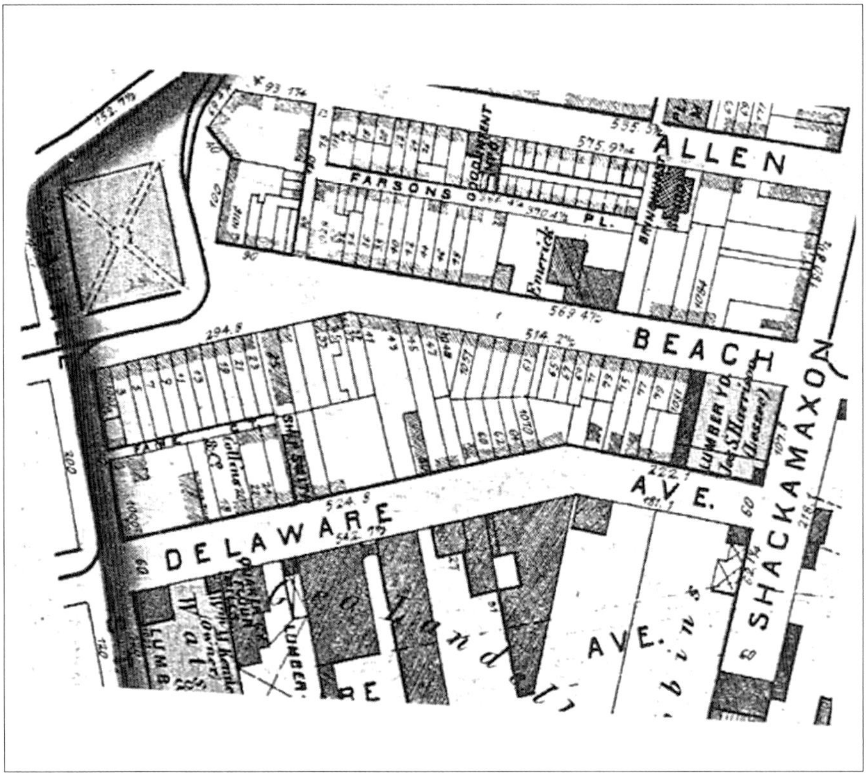

Shackamaxon Square, at the foot of Frankford Avenue and Beach Streets, is now obliterated by Delaware Avenue. G.M. Hopkins's Philadelphia Atlas of 1875.

Bromley's Atlas of 1922 shows only two small, green triangles left of the park—one that is cement today, and another that would have been somewhat catty-corner to today's cement island. The park was obliterated by Frankford Avenue, which cut directly through the center, and Delaware Avenue, running through its eastern edges.

It would be good to plant a tree and place a bench on that cement island, as a way of salvaging Shackamaxon Square's history

THE BRAMBLE CLUB

In the age before television and film, a look at the Bramble Club of Kensington offers insight into what local folks did for fun and entertainment.

The Bramble Club was a social organization made up of mainly businessmen from the Eighteenth Ward (Fishtown) of Kensington. It was formed in about February of 1889 to promote the interests of the neighborhood.

The club was very active in re-creations of historic anniversaries, such as William Penn's landing on the Delaware. This celebration would take place at Penn Treaty Park, which the club had been instrumental in helping to found. Besides the historical anniversary events in which the club participated, it was also keen on celebrating national holidays in the neighborhood, in particular, New Year's Day and the Fourth of July.

During the annual march of the Mummers Parade, the Bramble Club, in its early years, gave out several cash prizes to clubs who paraded in front of their clubhouse at 201 East Girard Avenue as incentive for the mummers to come to Kensington. The prizes were given for fancies, comics and bands. In those days, the mummers strutted all over the city, including down Girard Avenue.

One Fourth of July celebration sponsored by the Bramble Club had reenactments of the Boston Tea Party, the signing of the Declaration of Independence and Cornwallis's surrender. Another celebration of Independence Day had a parade with "upwards of twenty-five companies of boys' brigades, attached to the different churches led by the Bramble Club in full dress and the Yankee Doodle Band." The club also did reenactments of the signing of William Penn's Treaty.

Much of the organizing of the neighborhood for the celebration of these historic events, particularly those involving the youth of the local schools and churches, would be carried out by the Bramble Club and its members.

The purpose of recreating historical events was to keep the "Spirit of '76" alive, a reference to the glory days of the American Revolution, as many of the founders of the Bramble Club had ancestry that dated back to those days. When the club celebrated its ninth anniversary in February 1898, it was still an unchartered club. By 1918, the club was still active, having been in existence for nearly thirty years.

The "father" of the club was George T. Bramble, the son of a brass founder. Bramble was born in August of 1843 and probably died sometime in the 1920s. It is unclear just "how" Bramble came to be the founder and why the club was named for him. It may have been as simple as the fact that, in the early years, they met and had their clubhouse at Bramble's cigar store at 201 Girard Avenue (Shackamaxon and Girard).

The Girard Avenue residence of Bramble predates the founding of the club, as Bramble's parents, Joseph and Ann Bramble, are found living at 201 East Girard Avenue as early as 1880, if not earlier. Joseph Bramble was an old Kensington resident who worked in a brass foundry, while his son George worked at different jobs before settling into the cigar business.

There were at least two other Bramble families in the neighborhood at this time. It is unclear, however, just how they were related to each other, or to George T. Bramble.

George T. Bramble married a woman named Mary, and for whatever reason, the couple never had children. This quirk of life may have been the reason that George T. Bramble had the time to hang out with his friends in his cigar shop and help to found the Bramble Club.

The Bramble Club held its annual banquet and anniversary party on February 22, to honor George Washington's birthday. Onetime Eighteenth Ward city councilman and school board member William Rowan was the longtime president of the Bramble Club, and much of its success can be attributed to him. His family was one of the "Spirit of '76" families, having fought in the Revolutionary War. Besides Rowan, other local politicians were members—for example William F. Stewart, the local state representative.

At the club's sixth-anniversary banquet in 1896, there were 200 members present out of a reported 230 members. This large and solid organization of Kensington's business interests was the reason for the club's success. The celebrations of historical events that the club put on drew thousands of visitors from around the city and were reported regularly in the press.

BENJAMIN F. SHIBE

BASEBALL MAN

The real estate craze that is currently going on in the neighborhood is apparently claiming another historic site of Fishtown. The corner of Tulip and Palmer Streets, the place where A.J. Reach built his sporting goods empire and helped to put Fishtown and Kensington's stamp on Major League Baseball history, is currently being developed into residential units.

Over the last century or so, our neighborhood's connection to America's pastime has been through her native son Benjamin F. Shibe (1838–1922). Shibe was an early office man in Major League Baseball, a half owner and president of the famous Philadelphia Athletics club from 1901 until his death in 1922. It was the most successful sports franchise the city ever produced (nine pennants, five World Series).

Shibe was also partners with A.J. Reach in his sporting goods business, which, among other things, supplied baseballs to the major leagues. Historians have credited Ben Shibe with inventing cork-centered baseballs (patented in 1909) and the machinery used to make them. Today's baseball, the two-piece, stitched-leather design, is also credited to Shibe.

Ben Shibe was from the old part of Kensington known as Fishtown. He became an expert at leather working and carried on the business of making whips. His family lived in Fishtown and at least one member was originally a fisherman. When Shibe was starting out in the baseball business, he lived at 1053 East Norris Street.

With Shibe's knowledge of leather working, Reach thought Shibe would be a good fit for the ideas that he had about the emergence of the demand for sporting goods, and in about the year 1880, he approached Shibe about becoming a partner.

Reach had been a well-known baseball player in the early years of baseball (1860s–1870s), and he is credited by most as being the first "openly" paid professional baseball player. Baseball management recruited him in 1883 to become the owner and president of the Philadelphia Phillies, a new franchise in the recently formed National League.

Shibe was said to have been a bit of a sporting man himself. There was a local Kensington baseball club, called Shibe, founded sometime before the 1880s, but as yet, I cannot be sure if it was Ben's club. It was managed by Billy Sharsig, another Kensington fellow who appears to have played baseball, managed local clubs and was involved in the founding of the

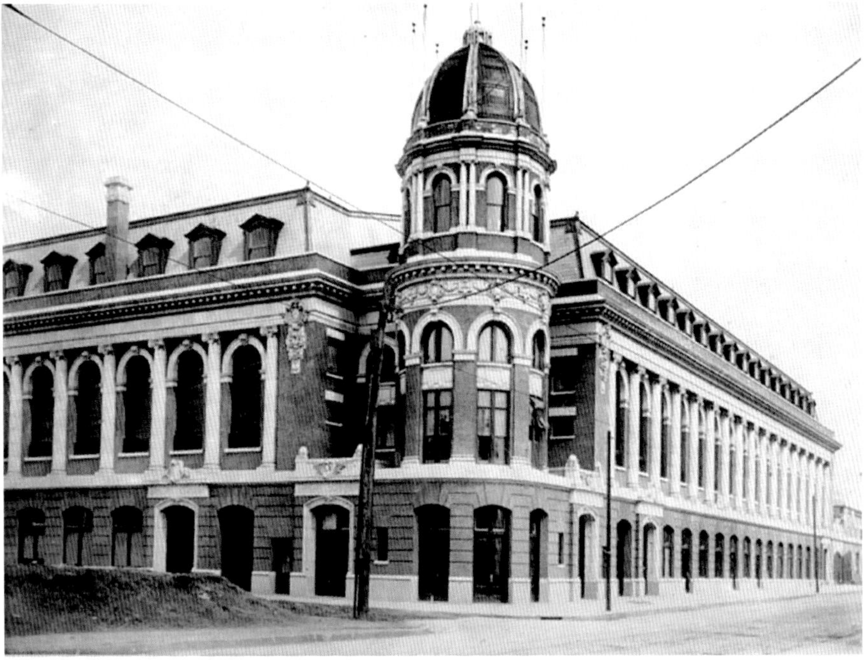

Shibe Park, circa 1913. Originally named for native Fishtowner Ben Shibe, it was later renamed Connie Mack Stadium. *Courtesy of the Library of Congress, George G. Bain Collection.*

American League. Sharsig eventually was picked by Shibe and Connie Mack to handle the financial affairs of the Philadelphia Athletics.

Soon after creating the partnership, Reach's new company opened up a plant at the northeast corner of Tulip and Palmer Streets, where they manufactured baseballs, baseball gloves, footballs and boxing gloves, as well as other sporting goods.

The original buildings of the company were erected about 1883, and when a Hexamer Survey was done in 1893, the company employed about 200 to 250 workers, with about 80 of them being females. Today, many, if not all, of the original buildings from the 1893 survey appear to be gone; however, you can still find some old-timers who can tell stories of sitting on the stoop stitching baseballs for the company.

Baseball legend Connie Mack approached Ben Shibe to become a half owner in Mack's team in the newly formed American League, called the Philadelphia Athletics. It is stated that Reach encouraged Shibe as a way of making sure their business interests would be secured in both leagues.

Ben Shibe, as the largest shareholder of the Athletics, became president of the club, with his son Tom being the vice-president and another son,

John, the secretary and business manager. Connie Mack was the treasurer and also controlled all the on-field aspects of the team.

In 1909, the Athletics played their first season in their new baseball stadium, Shibe Park, at 21st Street and Lehigh Avenue.

Shibe died in 1922. His son Tom took over the presidency of the club, and after his death in 1936, he was succeed by his brother John. John did not last long, resigning for health reasons by the end of the year. At this point, Connie Mack and his sons took full control of the ball club, both in the office and on the field.

In 1953, Shibe Park was renamed Connie Mack Stadium to honor the longtime owner/manager of the Athletics. Mack's family took over the ball team, buying out the remaining Shibe family members. In 1954, the Athletics left town for Kansas City, and later Oakland, California, and thus ended Fishtown's chapter in baseball history.

PART IV

INTERESTING NINETEENTH-CENTURY VIGNETTES

EARLIEST KNOWN USE OF THE NAME "FISHTOWN"

When the late Debbie Szumowski was editor of the *Fishtown Star*, I wrote a column for one of the Fishtown anniversary celebrations that she was so good at organizing. At that time, my research seemed to show that the name "Fishtown" had been around for at least 175 years, which pushed its origins back into the early to mid-1820s, thus discrediting the folktale that the English writer Charles Dickens had somehow named the area Fishtown. Dickens did not visit America for the first time until the year 1842, and Fishtown appeared to have already been known by its name for a number of years prior to his visit.

My research was based on a local newspaper I came across called *One Man News*, published in 1939. An article in that paper related the story of Jacob Faber, age seventy-eight, to whom, in 1878, when he was a lad of seventeen, a fellow named "Old Uncle Ben" related the original boundaries of Fishtown, that being the small area created by Susquehanna, Moyer, Montgomery, Richmond and Palmer Streets, with the Delaware River as the eastern border.

Old Uncle Ben stated that these boundaries were such when he was a young lad. From the name "Old Uncle Ben," I deducted that Old Uncle Ben's youth must have been at least back in the 1820s, assuming that someone with such a moniker would have been at least sixty to seventy years old. In either case, the name "Fishtown" would still predate Charles Dickens's first visit to Philadelphia in the 1840s, and thus disprove the folktale of Dickens naming the area. I wasn't totally happy with my conclusions, but they did seem to fit.

Well, I can happily state today that the name "Fishtown" actually dates from perhaps two decades prior to my original assumption—probably earlier!

I recently found a rather bizarre Philadelphia newspaper called *The Tickler*, rather satirical in nature, and published by one George Helmbold. In an issue dated November 16, 1808, I found the following article. (I might add that the italics were the publisher's, not mine.)

> *Scratch' em's Law Reports.*
> *Vol. I. Case V.*
>
> *In the Court of Common Pleas, a cause was tried on Tuesday the 8th, which excited considerable mirth.—The action was brought in due form of law…by plaintiff against defendant, for certain libelous expressions, of*

> *obscure though envious import. The plaintiff alleged and proved, that the defendant had, in the course of some gentle altercation, called her, horney Poll, and bristley Poll.*
>
> *Both plaintiff and defendant are females, and inhabitants of that eloquent part of the Northern suburbs, yelped Fish-town, and keep huckster shops in Market street. The court and jury were at a loss to perceive how horney Poll, and bristley Poll, could be considered as a libel on the plaintiff; but an explanation was given, which made the "men of law" shake their heads, and look wond'rous wise. Some years since, envy, malice, or some other foul passion, raised a report, that the plaintiff's husband had stolen a bullock, which he killed, and the plaintiff sold, reserving the horns for her own private use—defendant and others, in consequence, nicknamed her horney Poll. Motives equally base, had been exercised, in endeavoring to cast an odium on the plaintiff, by giving currency to a tale that she once went into a shop to purchase a bunch of bristles—that she paid for one and stole another bunch—hence the nickname of bristley Poll.*
>
> *The case was ably supported by counsel for plaintiff, who in very moving terms explained to the jury, the injurious tendency, a libel has to destroy the happiness and reputation of the aggrieved individual. The counsel for defendant admitted the use of the opprobrious terms and only pled in extenuation.*
>
> *The jury gave the plaintiff a verdict of 50 dollars, and costs, to silver over her horns and bristles.*

Of course, Helmbold seems to be having fun at the expense of Fishtowners, particularly due to the nature of the court case. His statement that the place is "yelped Fish-town" rather then "called Fishtown" pokes fun at the female fishmongers of the area, who, along with other family members, would have "yelped" their product at the fish market on Market Street, while their husbands or elder sons were out on the river plying their trade. Helmbold's mention of "the northern suburbs of Fish-town" is for now the earliest indication that I have found for the use of Fishtown's name.

I should note that Joe Walker, an old-time Fishtowner on Almond Street, called me the evening that this issue of the *Star* came out. He told me there was a mistake in my column, a spelling error. He thought the author probably wrote "ycleped" and not "yeleped" as I thought, or "yelped" as I transcribed. It seems that from Joe's background in the theater, he had come across this word on several occasions.

I reread the *The Tickler* article again, and it was as clear as day that the word was indeed "ycleped." "Ycelped" means "called," or "named," and it is described as being "obsolete, except in archaic or humorous writings."

Thus my claim that the use of "yelped" was a derogatory jab at the fishmonger women seems to have been misguided. The term "ycleped" was simply used to state that the place was "called" or "named" Fishtown. More importantly, the author's assertion that "that eloquent northern suburb" was called Fishtown remains the oldest known usage of this name for the neighborhood.

Native Fishtowners never cease to amaze me with their knowledge—in this case of an old archaic word, obsolete in its usage!

A PICTURE OF KENSINGTON IN 1811

In a book entitled *Stranger's Guide to Philadelphia*, published by a fellow named Paxton in the year 1811, we get an idea of what Kensington was like 197 years ago.

In 1811, Kensington contained 869 buildings, of which 52 were newly built. Of the total buildings, 664 or 76 percent were frame (wood) and only 205 were brick. There were 615 dwelling houses, 184 brick and 431 frame—70 percent of Kensington's inhabitants were living in wooden homes.

The business sector held one brick storehouse and eight frame ones. For manufacturing, there were five brick and five frame structures. There were only four public buildings, one brick and the other three frame. Presumably, one of the public buildings would have been the Kensington Methodist Episcopal Church, the only church built in the area at that time.

Stables and workshops made up a much larger part of the business sector. There were 231 stables and workshops, with 14 of these being brick and the rest (217) being frame. This means that, of the 869 buildings in Kensington, 27 percent were stables and workshops. Since stables and workshops were lumped together, and since owning a horse in those times was difficult, we can assume that most of the structures in this category were workshops and that Kensington would thus show strong small business beginnings.

With ten buildings being classified as manufacturing, some of them would have undoubtedly been the shipyards on the river run by the Bowers, Eyre, Grice, Vaughan and Van Dusen families, as well as the glasswork established before the Revolution at the north end of Kensington at about Dyott Street and the Delaware River. The old Governor's Mill at about today's 3rd and Girard was taken over in 1809 by a group of men led by Seth Craig. That same year, Charles B. Park opened his brass foundry in Kensington.

At this time, Kensington could boast of the Kensington Beneficial Society, headed by John Snyder, James Shellingsford and George Schoch, along with the Vanderslices (Jacob and Henry) and Enos Searles.

Medical needs were handled by several local midwives and nurses. County Physician for the Poor George Uhler came up to Kensington from the District of the Northern Liberties to administer to residents; otherwise they would have had to go into town for a doctor or hospital. There were no physicians listed in Kensington, nor were there any dentists, undertakers, leechers or bleeders.

Looking at maps of the period and street directories, we find that Kensington at this time had about thirty streets, alleys and roads. The streets of Kensington were mainly those that were within the triangle created by Frankford Road, Norris Street and the Delaware River. The area to the west, north of Girard Avenue, belonged, for the most part, to the large estates of the Masters and Norris families, and had not yet been totally broken up, sold off or developed. There was Mud Lane (Columbia Avenue), which went from Frankford Road to Germantown Road, and Timber Lane (Master Street), which ran west from Frankford Road. Additionally, there would have been some settlement along Germantown Road.

Beech Street ran along the coast of the Delaware River, from the bridge at the Cohocksink Creek (Poplar Street) to Gunnar's Run. The riverbank was lined with a few dozen wharves, which included about fifteen shipyards, along with allied businesses like mast makers and lumberyards. The shipyards ran from Poplar Street up to about Palmer Street, at which point the area along the river north of Palmer would have been inhabited by the fishermen. This area was the original Fishtown.

Compared to other outlying districts, Kensington was about a fifth the size of Northern Liberties (4,280 buildings) and a third the size of Southwark (2,739 buildings). Of course, Northern Liberties and Southwark both lay adjacent to the old city proper and thus one could have expected them to grow faster prior to Kensington's creation.

When you look at the justices of the peace, the constables and the county commissioners for the Northern Liberties Township, there are not any recognizable Kensingtonians, except Samuel Grice. At this time, Kensington was still under the control of the Northern Liberties Township, which was dominated by men from the District of the Northern Liberties. This was one of the main reasons that Kensington petitioned the state for independent status, and in 1820, Kensington became a self-governed district, remaining so until 1854, when the whole of Philadelphia County was incorporated into the city of Philadelphia.

Edgar Allan Poe Reports on Kensington in 1840

Clarence S. Brigham, in his book *Edgar Allan Poe's Contributions to Alexander's Weekly Messenger*, states that Poe wrote about the Kensington railroad riots in that publication on March 18, 1840. In an article entitled "The Rail Road War," Poe gives us his interpretation of this often-overlooked Kensington event.

> *During the last ten days, or thereabouts, the sober inhabitants of the District of Kensington have been all alive with a delightful little war of their own—a nice rough-and-tumble affair—none of your bloodhound business, or Bugaboo and Kickapoo campaigns. The Philadelphia and Trenton Rail-road Company had received permission, it seems, from one of our judicial tribunals, to lay their rails in Front street, but could not obtain the consent of the property holders of the region. For some time past the work has been going on, however, with much grumbling and many threats on the part of the Front-streeters, but with no overt act of resistance. On Monday morning, about ten o'clock, matters took the first serious turn. Quite a mob—men, women, and children—surrounded the laborers at the rails; replacing the paving-stones which had been displaced, and otherwise interrupting the work. The sheriff was sent for, arrived about 12, with his posse, and arrested Henry Rowan, John Craydon, and Francis Farley… The arrest of these persons intimidated the crowd for a time, but in the afternoon the riot again commenced. About 4 o'clock Hugh Lemon was arrested, taken before the Mayor, and bound over in the sum of $300.*
>
> *On Tuesday and Wednesday the excitement still continued, and a great number of the gentle engaged in the melee. On Thursday the disorders increased. Mr. Naglee was violently assaulted with paving stones discharged from the fair hands of the damsels of Kensington, who also led away in triumph a wagon containing iron rails for the road, the laborers being fairly driven off the ground. Many arrests were made, but with no good effect. In the afternoon the Sheriff and his whole posse were routed, and the rioters, having beaten them off, proceeded to tear up that portion of the road which was the nearest to completion; disengaging not only the rails but the wooden frames, and filling up the excavations with dirt and stones. In the meantime placards were posted up calling upon the people to "put down the rail-road nuisance," and addressed especially to the firemen, draymen and carters—who were invited to attend a meeting on Thursday evening,*

> *in the Commissioners Hall, Kensington. The meeting was accordingly held, and served, as a matter of course, to inflame the wrath of the mob, who adjourned to the scene of action, and set fire to the timber intended for the road. The Judges of the Court of Quarter Sessions now issued a general warrant, authorizing the Sheriff to command the service of every able-bodied citizen to aid in quelling the disturbances. This officer issued notices accordingly, and gave directions to the whole police force, as well as to all the watchmen, to meet at his office on Friday. But before the time appointed, the Rail-road Company had agreed to discontinue the laying of the rails until the decision of the Supreme Court could be obtained...An announcement of the Company's submission was duly made by the Sheriff to the mob, who first raised an uproarious shout of triumph, and then dispersed in high glee. Thus ended the great rail-road war.*

While Poe tells us the "great rail-road war" ended in March 1840, in fact it dragged out until June of 1842, and there were outbursts at least "four different times between 2 March 1840 and 3 February 1841."

The residents along Front Street, between Girard and Montgomery, didn't want a railroad down their street. The ashes and sparks of the railroad created a hazardous environment for wooden homes and stores,

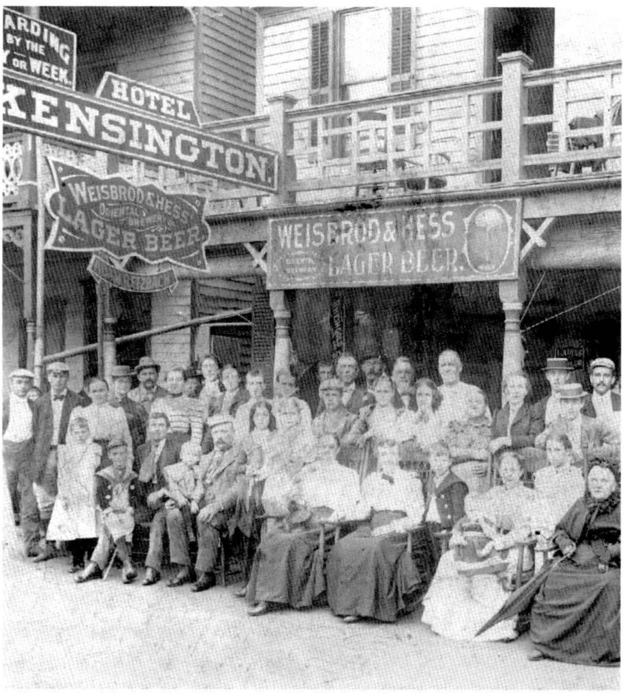

The Kensington Hotel, on Front and Palmer Streets, circa 1882–1910, opposite the Kensington Railroad Depot, near where the railroad riots took place.

not to mention the danger to the neighborhood children. There was also the disruption to the local drayman and carter's cross-street traffic. Every time the railroad's workmen showed up, they were driven off. Even Emery's Tavern at Front and Phoenix (Thompson), the sheriff's posse's headquarters, was torched and burnt down. The building of the railroad became a struggle between "Popular Rights" and "Monopoly Capitalism," and this time popular rights won out. The railroad gave up and the state legislature gave in—the railroad was not built. Ironically enough, eighty years later SEPTA's Frankford elevated train, "the El," was built down Front Street.

USS *ALLIGATOR*

FIRST SUBMARINE OF THE UNITED STATES NAVY

On the small hill along the Memphis Street side of Fishtown's Palmer Cemetery sit a number of tombstones packed rather closely together. The gravestones belong to the Eakins and Moser families, with one belonging to Christiana Moser, a local Fishtown girl, the daughter of a butcher, who had married a downtown fellow named Samuel Eakins. They married in the year 1830, at First Presbyterian Church of Kensington, and made their home on Palmer Street, near Richmond.

While the tombstones look rather ordinary, they represent a small piece of a fascinating story, which only now is becoming known. That story is about the USS *Alligator*, the first submarine of the United States Navy.

Recently, I was contacted by a retired navy man to do some genealogical research on his ancestor, Samuel Eakins. Eakins had married the Moser girl from Fishtown. As it turns out, Samuel Eakins was the first acting master of a naval submarine in the history of the United States Navy. A major effort by various government agencies and private organizations is underway to try to find the *Alligator*, which sank in the Atlantic Ocean during the Civil War. My client was putting together the biography of Eakins to go along with the underwater archaeological investigations that are currently in progress.

The creator of the *Alligator* was a French immigrant, Brutus de Villeroi, a self-described genius (as evidenced in the U.S. census, where he states such as his occupation). Villeroi had a history in submarines dating back to 1830s

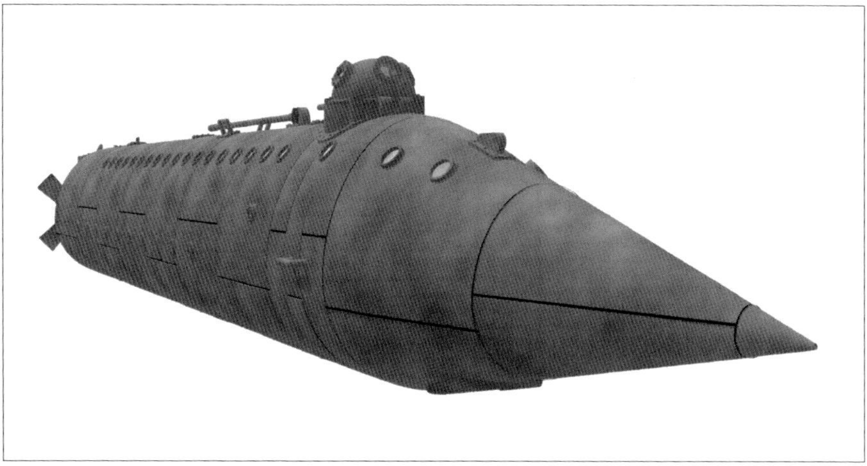

The first U.S. Navy submarine, USS *Alligator*, was built at the Kensington shipyard of Neafie and Levy. It was launched on May 2, 1862. *Courtesy of the U.S. Navy.*

France, where it is stated that he was the math teacher for none other than Jules Verne, the science fiction writer famed for the book *Twenty Thousand Leagues Under the Sea*, published in 1870 and featuring a submarine.

Villeroi contacted the American government upon arriving in Philadelphia in 1861. He was actually taken into custody by Philadelphia's harbor police when he tried sailing one of his "infernal machines" (a submarine) up the Delaware River during the early stages of the Civil War.

After explaining his ideas and receiving permission to go ahead with his project of building a sub, he contracted for the government with the Kensington shipyard of Neafie and Levy for the construction of "one iron submarine" in November of 1861. The Neafie and Levy shipyard sat where the PECO plant is today, just north of Penn Treaty Park.

According to naval historians, the *Alligator* was

> *the most technologically advanced weapon in the Union naval arsenal, incorporating technology not usually associated with the Civil War Navy: a diver's airlock, tanks of compressed air for adjusting the altitude of the boat, a large crew of twenty men, and an air scrubbing system to remove carbon dioxide from the atmosphere. Its mode of attack—electrically-detonated limpet mines placed by its diver.*

By early May 1862 the submarine was launched. It was forty feet long, six feet high and four and a half feet wide, and painted green, hence the name *Alligator*. In June 1862, Samuel Eakins was put in charge as the acting master.

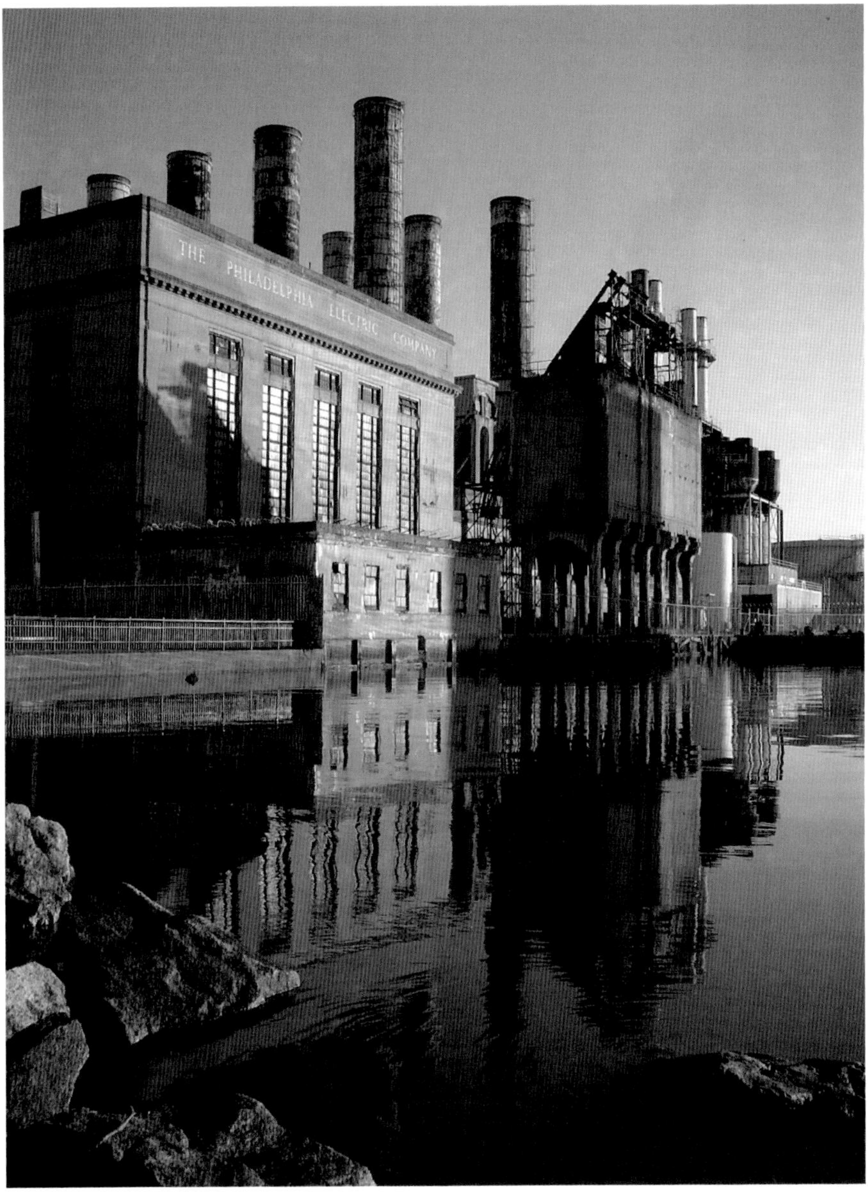

North of Penn Treaty Park, the site of the former Neafie and Levy shipyard. Philadelphia Electric built this coal-fired power station in 1920. *Courtesy Torben Jenk.*

During the summer and winter of 1862, the *Alligator* had a civilian crew, with Eakins in charge. Eakins, a civilian himself, had a background as a diver and had previously worked for the czar of Russia, salvaging Russian ships that had been lost during the Crimean War.

In the early spring of 1863, the *Alligator* was given the assignment to destroy underwater obstacles that were blocking and barring the waters around the port of Fort Sumter in Charleston Harbor. While the *Alligator* was being towed toward its destination for its assignment, a violent storm erupted around Cape Hatteras, North Carolina, already known as the "graveyard of the Atlantic" due to all the ships that had been lost in that area. During this storm the *Alligator* was cut loose, so as not to cause the ship and crew that was towing it to sink, and thus the life of the *Alligator* came to an end at the bottom of the Atlantic.

Villeroi, the *Alligator*'s creator, died in 1875, and his more advanced technology of submarines died with him. The United States' interest in submarines would not be revisited for the next forty years.

This fascinating story of the USS *Alligator* can be read about more deeply at the website of the Office of Naval Research and the National Oceanic and Atmospheric Administration (http://sanctuaries.noaa.gov/alligator/).

These two groups are spearheading a project to raise the submarine from the floor of the Atlantic, just as soon as it is located. You can also read about the hunt for the *Alligator* at the Navy and Marine Living History Association's website, which has a number of excellent illustrations (http://www.navyandmarine.org/alligator/index.htm).

A LOOK AT FRANKFORD AVENUE IN 1890

In 1891, a fellow named Stephen Baxindine published a book called *Kensington: City Within a City. An Historical and Industrial Review.* The title is a little misleading, as it is really a small business directory for Kensington. There is a brief 12-page history of Kensington, but the rest of the 588-page book is filled with short, half- or full-page biographies of local businesses. Baxindine wrote over 650 extremely informative business biographies of the small businesses in Kensington, particularly along routes like Frankford Avenue, which was once a great business district. Long dormant, it has recently started to show signs of revitalization.

In 1890, Frankford Avenue below Girard Avenue did not have that many small businesses, as it was taken up by larger manufacturers. The 900 block had a saddlery and harness place; a dealer in feed, grain, hay, straw and salt; boarding stables; and a grocery. The 1000 block had three carriage or wagon builders and another saddlery and harness business, and the 1100 block had a window shade manufacturer.

Above Girard Avenue, at the 1200 block, there started to be a change in the businesses. That first block above Girard had a couple of furniture manufacturers and a Presbyterian Church, and then on the 1300 block, there was an upholstery and chair business. A grocery, bakery and blacksmith's shop were also available to folks, and if you smoked, you could get your cigars from Henry Fluer's "Singing Birds, and Cigars."

The 1400 block was more industrial, with a color grinder, paint and wood filler manufacturer, but there was also a wholesale and retail cigar shop, a laundry, a blacksmith's shop and a hardware shop.

The 1500 and 1600 blocks were not represented, being residential.

At the 1700 block, the business district started to set in with various businesses: a tonsorial parlor, dry goods and notions, cigars and tobacco, wallpaper and decorations, watchmakers and jewelers, men's furnishings,

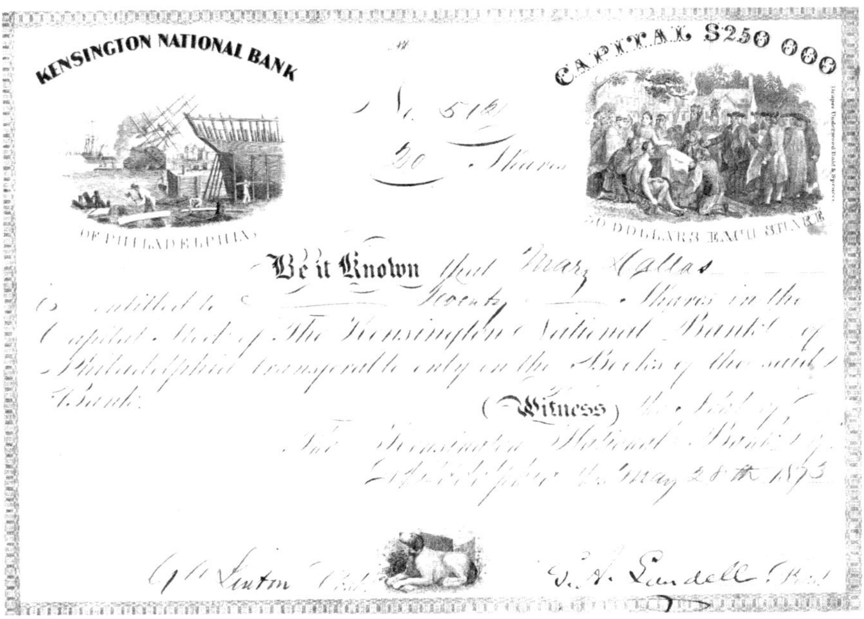

A stock certificate of Kensington National Bank (Frankford and Girard) showing vignettes of the shipbuilding industry and Penn's Treaty, pieces of the neighborhood's history.

a milk depot and a grocery and provisioner. There was even a secondhand furniture store.

The 1800 block had the homes of three local ministers from neighborhood churches, as well as a fourth on the previous block. The 1800 block also had the Kensington Beef Market and Joseph Nicholls's "Oyster Bay."

There was no 1900 block. Due to bends in the Delaware River and the fact that the neighborhood is along the riverbank, the address system is sometimes cockeyed.

The heart of the lower Frankford Avenue business district was between the 2000 block and the 2600 block, where there were upwards of seventy-five businesses listed (minus the 2100 block, which also did not exist).

The 2000 block had house furnishings, heaters and ranges, picture frames and art, secondhand goods, a tonsorial artist, a boot and shoemaker, a photographer, pianos, organs, musical instruments and sheet music.

The 2200 block had furniture, bedding, house furnishings, two shoe stores and another wholesale and retail cigar, tobacco and pipe shop.

The 2300 block offered ice cream and confectionary; fancy goods and notions; two more shoe and boot stores; another candy shop specializing in fine caramels; a china, glass and "Queensware" shop; a men's furnishing store; a bakery; and yet another tobacco shop.

The 2400 block had a "fine watch" and jewelry shop; a tailor; a saddle, harness, collar and whip manufacturer; a millinery; a pinking and stamping business; an interior decorator and upholsterer; and another house goods store. There was also on this block "The Great Atlantic & Pacific Tea, Co., Importers of Coffee Roasters and Retail Dealers in Teas and Coffee"; another tonsorial artist; a fine stationary store; a hatter; a "Gent's" furnishing store; more china, glassware, and home furnishings; and a second tea dealer, the "Assam China and Japan Tea Company, Wholesale and Retail Dealers in Teas, Coffees and Fancy Groceries."

The 2400 block also had a local "Book, Card and Job Printer," another millinery and a hatter.

The 2500 block started with the "Globe Meat Market"; "Harrison's, Cigars and Tobacco, Stationery and Music" store; an English clog manufacturer; a hardware store; another "Dry Goods and Notions" shop; a butcher; another millinery; more boots and shoes; fancy and staple groceries; and a wholesale liquor dealer and rectifier.

The 2600 block had an interior decorations store; a cigar and tobacco shop; an ice cream and confectionery place; more tobacco, boots and shoes; a gentlemen's furnishing store; notions and trimmings; and carpets and oil cloths "on installments."

There were only about eight or so businesses that were listed above the 2600 block of Frankford Avenue, showing that Kensington at that time really was considered to be concentrated south of Lehigh Avenue.

As you can imagine, there was an incredible amount of goods and services available on Frankford Avenue a hundred years ago. With ideas of bringing back the avenue, we can only hope that the new artisans in the area keep these storefronts for the public and resist turning them into private homes.

KENSINGTON'S ELITE ADDRESSES OF THE 1890S

In Philadelphia, before the *Social Register* was published, there was the *Boyd's Philadelphia Blue Book*. Starting around 1880, this annual publication listed Philadelphia's elite and social climbers. The volume for March 1893 states that it includes "25,000 prominent householders."

In many cases, pedigree counted more than money at that time, and along with guides like the *Social Register* and *Boyd's Blue Book*, there was also much activity in the formation of lineage societies, which allowed elites to identify one another among the seemingly endless waves of immigrants. Organizations like the Daughters of the Revolution and the Mayflower Society helped to identify who was who in the ever-changing social scene of America, as "new money" families tried to enter the upper class of society.

What I like about these books is that you can identify certain blocks in Kensington where the "elites" congregated in the nineteenth century. For example, when I was a child there used to be large, three-story homes on Cumberland Street from Jasper to Emerald Street. Today, most of those homes have been torn down and remain empty lots, but back in 1893, this was an elite block in Kensington with five homes listed on the south side of Cumberland Street. One home belonged to George Weisbrod (1924 East Cumberland), a partner in Weisbrod and Hess Brewery, a local concern where the Philadelphia Brewing Company is today.

Farther east on Cumberland, between Frankford and Tulip Streets, there are eight households listed. At 2209 East Cumberland lived the famed toy manufacturer Albert Schoenhut, and on the same block was the Reverend John A. Goodfellow, longtime pastor of the Episcopal Church of the Good

Shepherd (Collins and Cumberland Streets), where he served for a record sixty-one years (1872–1933).

The 2300 block of east Cumberland had eleven homes listed, including the Harbison dairy family (2345 East Cumberland) and Christian Hess (2357 East Cumberland), the other partner in the Weisbrod and Hess Brewery.

In all, Cumberland between Jasper and Gaul Streets had twenty-nine homes listed in the book, the most of any street in the Kensington area. The next runner-up was North 6th Street, which had twenty-four households, many of them "new money" German and German-Jewish families who congregated on the western border of Kensington.

The big homes that lined the streets of Norris Square were highly represented (Hancock Street, nineteen houses; Howard Street, eighteen houses; Susquehanna Avenue, sixteen houses; Diamond Street, six houses), as was the business district along Frankford Avenue (eighteen families).

The same street addresses that are bringing big money in the gentrification of Fishtown today were also good blocks in 1893: 900–1200 Shackamaxon (twelve homes), 2300 block Dauphin (seven homes), 1000–1400 Columbia

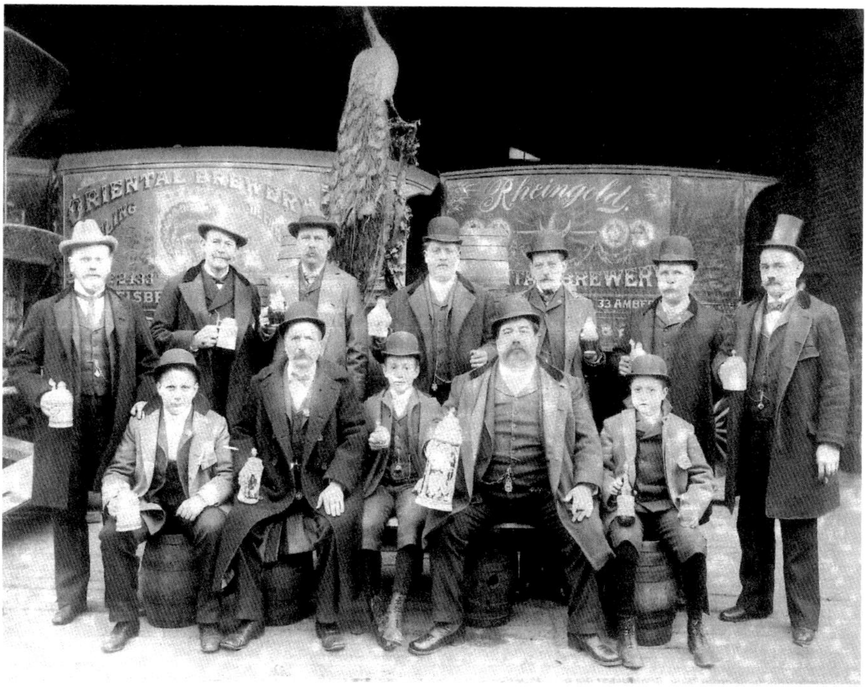

Weisbrod and Hess Oriental Brewery. *Bottom row, left to right*: George Weisbrod Jr., Christian Hess, William Weisbrod, George Weisbrod Sr. and Frederick Hess.

(thirteen homes) and 1000–1400 Marlborough (fifteen homes). However, Montgomery Avenue, a very fine street today, only had six houses listed—four on the 1300 block and two on the 1500 block. Palmer Street had lumber merchant Alexander Adaire at 1414 and baseball man Ben Shibe's relatives at 1311. Richmond Street and Beach Streets, places that used to house Kensington's elites during the first three quarters of the nineteenth century, now only had ten homes represented between them.

Lehigh Avenue, a rather new street for Kensington, but a fancy street when it was laid out, had eighteen homes listed between 5th and 9th Streets. My own York Street was represented with nine homes, most of them on the 2200 and 2300 blocks. My own home was occupied by Samuel Creighton, the vice-president/treasurer of Dungan, Hood and Company, a large morocco leather manufactory at American and Dauphin Streets.

Other streets not mentioned above, but represented in *Boyd's Blue Book* of 1893 were the 2000 block Amber, 1200–2100 Germantown, 2400–2500 Kensington, 300 block Norris, 100 block Oxford, 1000–2400 North Front, 900–2500 North 2nd, 2000–2400 North Third, 1300–1500 North 4th and 1200–1600 North 5th.

At this time (1893), Kensington had 125,000 residents, but only 360 families are represented in *Boyd's Blue Book*. They were manufacturers, industrialists, bankers, clergy and politicians, but they were our citizens as well, since no matter their worth, it was a time when the wealthy lived among the working class.

The movement of the upper class out of the neighborhood started before 1893, as many of Kensington's elites had begun to move to the "new money" neighborhood of North Broad Street (Broad to 20th, Girard to Diamond). By the end of World War I (1918), the movement of the elites out of the neighborhood was almost complete. Now, elites that lived outside of the neighborhood would control Kensington's institutions and factories, and as the next generation took over these institutions, there was no longer the connection to the neighborhood by the founders of these businesses that had once existed. Thus, a large part of what made Kensington great was lost.

THE COHOCKSINK CREEK

KENSINGTON'S HISTORICAL BORDER

Recently I was down at Liberty Lands Park, the small park that sits on the site of the old Burk Brothers Leather Works between 3rd and Bodine Streets, just north of Poplar Street. On the south side of the park is a nice mural by a fellow named Dennis Haugh that prominently features the old Cohocksink Creek. The mural, a project that was in the works for quite a while, was finally finished and dedicated recently.

It makes sense that the Cohocksink Creek is featured in the mural, as Liberty Lands Park sits on the southern bank of the old creek. The creek actually still runs right there underneath Bodine Street, but long ago it was made into a canal, then a culvert and then paved over and made into a sewer that runs beneath the street.

Historically, the creek served as the southern border for Kensington. There was a pond that fed the creek at about where the playground is today, above 5th and Thompson Streets. The creek flowed down Orkney Street to Cambridge Street, then down Cambridge Street to Bodine Street, down Bodine Street to Laurel Street and across Laurel Street at 2nd Street. From there it wound its way up Hancock Street to Allen Street, down Allen Street, crossed in front of Immaculate Conception Roman Catholic Church, and finally reached Canal Street and wound its way to the Delaware River, emptying into the river just below Poplar Street.

Today, many of the new residents in the area call the neighborhood along the "northern" bank of the old creek Northern Liberties, but actually it is Kensington. You won't find any old map stating differently. You can't fault the new folks—they don't know any better. They were probably told the area was the Northern Liberties by some real estate agent, but there are folks still living that call it Kensington, yours truly being one of them.

I tend not to pay much attention to the real estate people when they start changing the name of a neighborhood. Just look at what is happening right now in Fishtown. Fishtown is a hot neighborhood for real estate. Houses are bringing high values like they never have before. In order to cash in on these high prices, realtors and speculators are starting to expand the traditional boundaries of Fishtown in hopes of being able to sell homes to folks who are looking to buy into a booming real estate neighborhood, and those new residents will proudly go along and call the area they moved into by the name that the realtor told them.

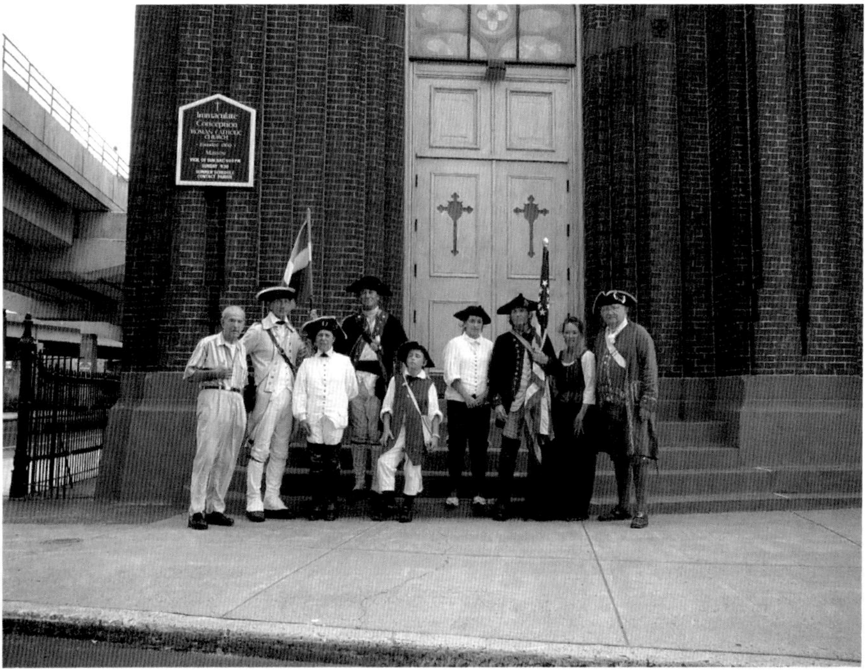

In September 2006, 225 years after Washington and Rochambeau's march to Yorktown, reenactors marched through Kensington, greeting Judge Lederer at Immaculate Conception Church. *Courtesy Torben Jenk.*

If you have read the advertisements for real estate lately, you have probably noticed that houses on Cumberland Street, Huntingdon Street and even Lehigh Avenue are now being marketed as part of Fishtown. They were always part of Kensington, or perhaps Port Richmond, depending on what block they were, but never Fishtown. I even saw some advertisements by realtors that were calling the factory district around Front and York Streets by the name of Fishtown. How blasphemous is that!

The same thing that is happening to Fishtown happened to Northern Liberties just a short time ago. When I was a child, my family lived at 1141 Germantown Avenue (now the loading dock for the paint store), and Schmidt's Brewery was just out our back door. We always called the area Kensington. I asked my mother what it was called when she was a kid (1930s–1940s) and she said Kensington. But along comes someone like Bart Blatstein, with his various development projects, and he calls the area the Northern Liberties. Of course, to be fair to Bart, the artists and realtors were already calling the area the Northern Liberties before he got there—so perhaps he didn't know either.

The old Schmidt's Brewery site, which Blatstein is developing, is clearly in Kensington, as old records show it was once called the Kensington Brewery, not to mention the fact that it is far north of the Cohocksink Creek. Blatstein's project, called "Artists Walk," is also clearly located in Kensington, as it sits next to Schmidt's, above Wildey, between 2nd and Bodine Streets.

Other developers have done the same thing. The Cigar Factory condominiums over at 4th and Cambridge Streets are in Kensington, as is Waterfront Square, the five towers that are being built on the 900 block of Penn Street, on the Delaware River just north of Poplar Street. However, both of these projects are advertised as the Northern Liberties.

I suppose we can consider ourselves lucky; lucky in the sense that since Fishtown is now a hot market, the Northern Liberties neighborhood won't be expanding anymore. However, now large chunks of Port Richmond are quickly becoming Fishtown, and Kensington keeps being decimated.

PART V

STORIES OF CEMETERIES, CHURCHES AND HOSPITALS

WEST STREET BURIAL GROUND

The cemetery sat four feet above grade and "foul oozings from the ground poured out upon the pavement," creating "an intolerable stench," which was "compelling the people to abandon their properties." Those who still resided across from the cemetery "resided there with their windows closed."

A newspaper reporter described the above scene of a Fishtown cemetery in 1885. The cemetery the reporter came to write about was the old West Street Burial Ground, also known as Union Burial Ground, Malt House Ground, German Burial Ground and Thumlert's.

The cemetery was located on the south side of Vienna Street between West and Gaul Streets. In today's parlance, it would have been the lot of ground that is taken up by the top halves of the two blocks between Montgomery and Berks Streets and Gaul and Belgrade Streets, which have Miller Street running between them.

The cemetery dates to 1831, when a group of men from the Northern Liberties founded it. The trustees all had been previously involved with a group called the Union Burial Ground Association. The Union Burial Ground Association ran the cemetery from its inception in 1831 to 1851, when it conveyed the unoccupied ground to Joseph R. Dickson with the stipulation that the land be used for burial purposes. Dickson died in the late 1860s, when a fellow named Magargee was found to be handling his estate.

There were some veterans of the Civil War buried at the cemetery, as there is mention in 1874 of the GAR's Walter S. Newhall Post, No. 7, coming to the cemetery during their annual parade marches to pay respect to fallen soldiers.

By the late 1870s, the cemetery fell into decline, and the actual ownership was called into doubt. Philadelphia's Board of Health declared the cemetery a nuisance in 1876. In addition to the stench mentioned above, family and friends were removing bodies and not filling the graves back in.

At a meeting of lot holders in 1877, a committee was formed to handle some of the complaints. Money was raised, a fence erected and flowers planted.

The cosmetic repairs had no effect, as the neighbors across from the cemetery were complaining to the city the next year. The cemetery was again declared a nuisance, and by 1879, people were asked to remove the remains of their loved ones.

In 1885, when the newspaper reporter mentioned above showed up, the neighbor he interviewed stated that the vandals in the neighborhood destroyed the place:

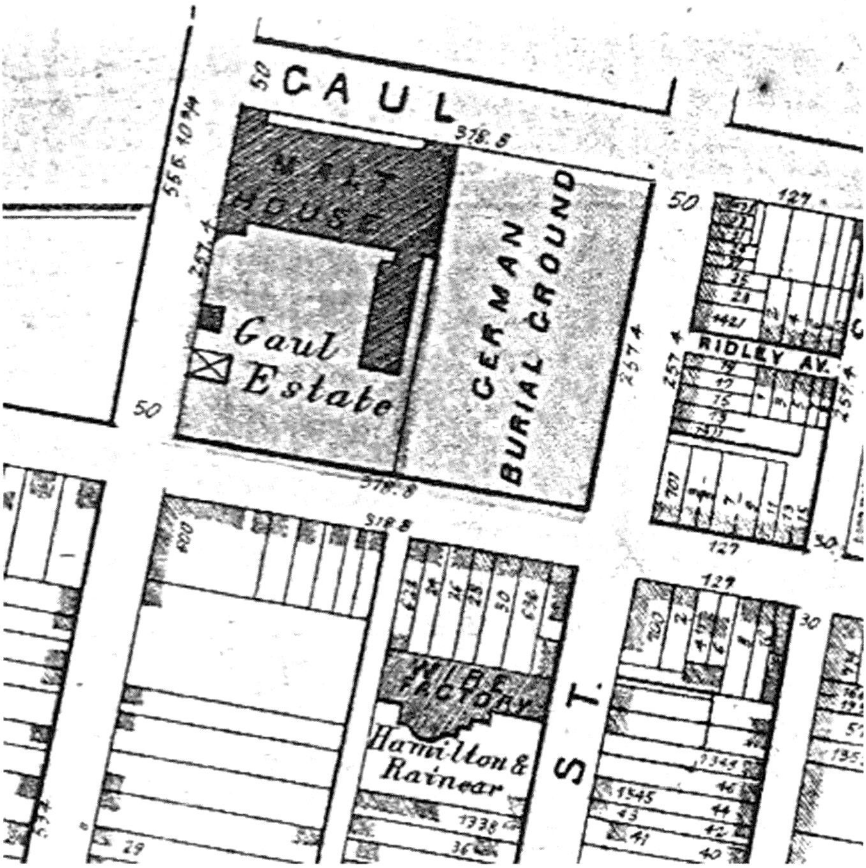

West Street Burial Ground (German Burial Ground), between Gaul and Belgrade and Montgomery and Berks. *G.M. Hopkins's Atlas of 1875.*

> *We have some powerful bad boys in this neighborhood. They got at the fence, and now, as you see, there's nothing left but the posts, and they have dug up most of them…One lady had a brother lying there. She went to his grave to have him taken up. They opened it and found not one coffin, but six. The lady said to put 'em all back again; she didn't know which coffin was her brother's, or whether he was there at all…The people about here used to be afraid to pass it at night for fear of ghosts.*

The reporter finished his story on the cemetery with the following comments:

> *Thus spoke the resident, and in view of the neglect into which their long home had been suffered to fall, it did not seem wholly unreasonable to imagine it haunted, not by one ghost only, but by an entire indignation meeting of specters.*

In 1892, the cemetery was sold and the lingering remains were removed to Northwood Cemetery. In 1936, a fellow named J.E. Sturgis Nagle stated that "when they removed the dead…they dug up the bodies of soldiers, and the diggers gave the buttons from the uniforms to children."

The history of this cemetery is a classic example of the effects of absentee ownership of property. Palmer Cemetery was founded nearly a hundred years prior to West Street and is still burying people today, whereas West Street lasted fewer than fifty years. The fact that the founders and trustees of West Street were from the Northern Liberties, and not Kensington, played a major role in the cemetery's decline, as there was not the same connection to the West Street Ground by its neighbors as there was/is to Palmer Cemetery, which was always controlled by residents of Kensington.

Eventually, Miller Street was cut through the cemetery, with two blocks of homes built on top of the old burial grounds and Gaul's Malt House lot to the south. So today, if you happen to live in these homes and you smell a foul odor coming from your basement, it just might be more than your sewer backing up.

HANOVER BURIAL GROUNDS

Like the West Street Burial Ground, the Hanover Street Burial Grounds is an ancient cemetery that used to sit where Hetzell's Playground is today; that is, the area bordered by Hanover Street (today's Columbia Avenue), Thompson, Livingston and Earl Streets. The cemetery was actually three cemeteries in one—Kensington Methodist Episcopal, Union Harmony Burial Company and Union Wesleyan Church.

The Kensington Methodist Episcopal lot was purchased in 1805 by Methodist Episcopal of Philadelphia and transferred to Kensington ME (Old Brick) Church in 1809. The Board of Health Registers has records of their burials as early as the years 1838–1858, but undoubtedly there were earlier ones.

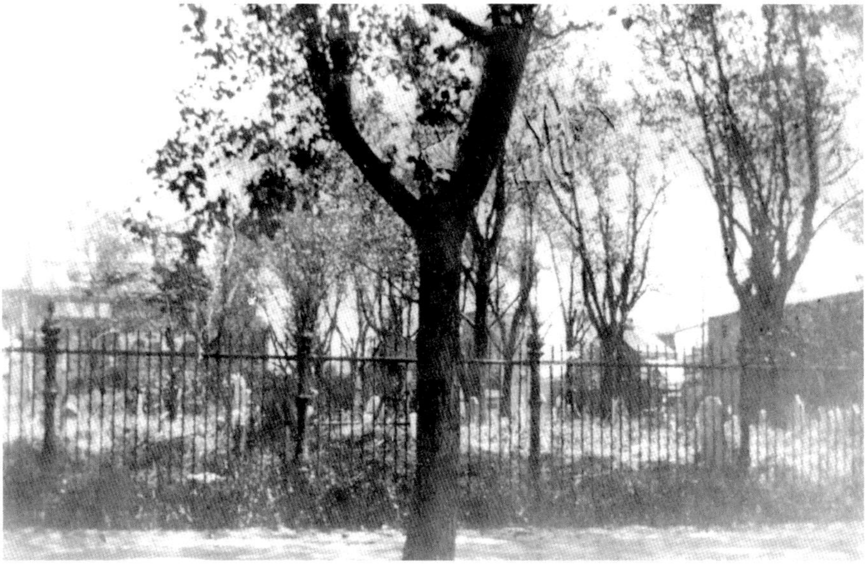

Hanover Street Burial Grounds, facing north on Columbia Avenue, west of Thompson Street, is the site of Hetzell's Playground today.

The Union Harmony Burial Company ground was purchased in 1828. In 1831, Union Wesleyan Church Burial Company purchased and incorporated the southern portion of the lot. The Philadelphia Board of Health Registers had Harmony Burial Company burials listed as early as 1828 1831.

The cemetery first appeared in 1849 on J.C. Sidney's *Map of the City of Philadelphia.*

When Hanover Street Burial Grounds closed in about 1922–1923, the remains of Kensington Methodist Episcopal are said to have been removed to Forest Hills Cemetery (Delaware County, Pennsylvania). The remains of Union Harmony Burial Company and Union Wesleyan Church Burial Company were removed to section thirty of Fernwood Cemetery (Montgomery County, Pennsylvania).

It was also reported that there were some remains removed to Graceland Cemetery (Yeadon, Pennsylvania). Additionally, it has been reported that there were some bodies removed to North Cedar Hill Cemetery, in Philadelphia. Unfortunately, there also have been some remains found from time to time when Hetzell's Playground gets renovated, as recently as a year or so ago.

George R. Barker, who did research on this cemetery back in the 1940s, talked with local contractor George Vaughn, of East Montgomery Street, who told him that some tombstones from Hanover Street Burial Grounds were used in constructing some of the homes on Susquehanna Avenue, presumably as foundation stones. If you live on Susquehanna, you might want to check your basement for signs of this story being true.

Hanover was also known as "Helverson's Grounds" and "Helverson's Burying Ground," after Nicholas Helverson (b. ca. 1789, d. bef. 1860), a "furnishing undertaker & coffin maker" at the southeast corner of Coates (Fairmount) and Saint John's (American) Streets, down in the Northern Liberties. He was also listed as the superintendent of several burying grounds elsewhere in the city, as is evidenced by the "Helverson's Grounds" on Frankford Road (Avenue) in 1855, which would have been a part of today's Shissler, or Newt's Playground. Philadelphia's Board of Health Registers of 1845–46 reports a "Helverson's Ground," and the Second Universalist Church's register mentions "funerals & other grounds" in an 1855 internment at "Helverson's Ground on Frankford Road."

In some Fishtown and Kensington obituaries, you'll find mention of the deceased being placed in the Hanover Vault, which was a holding place for the deceased. It does not necessarily mean that the person was buried at the cemetery. They could have been placed there during the winter months, since they lived locally, and then were buried elsewhere when the ground was soft enough to dig and bury the body.

If you visit my website (www.kennethwmilano.com) there are several photographs and a map of the cemetery (click on the Encyclopaedia Kensingtoniana link and then on the Church and Cemetery link). The photographs show the cemetery and the vault, and there is a nice photograph that shows a row of old, wooden, ramshackle homes that lined the west side of Thompson Street between Columbia (then Hanover) and Earl Streets. These homes were only about half the width of a normal house and look like wooden Father–Son–Holy Ghost houses (trinities). I am guessing that these homes were built to subsidize the cemetery, perhaps as rental units. They were torn down in 1923 after the cemetery was removed and the whole area was replaced by Hetzell's Playground, which still exists at this site today.

Hetzell's Playground was named for Isaac D. Hetzell, a local contractor who lived at 322 Richmond Street. Hetzell followed his father Andrew into the bricklaying and paving business (A. Hetzell and Company), eventually becoming a substantial contractor. He parlayed his money and influence into a councilman seat in city government, where he served for a number of years.

EARLY WORSHIP IN KENSINGTON

When Palmer Cemetery was first established in the middle of the eighteenth century, Kensington already had a large German population. The open, grassy area that sits on the Palmer Street side of the cemetery, where the veteran's monument now stands, was originally an area that had been set aside to build a school for the English and German languages, as dictated by the Palmer family when they gave the land to the community for the cemetery.

There were no churches at this point in Kensington's history. The Germans of the area had to go into town, to Saint Michael's (5th Street and Appletree Alley) or Zion (4th and Cherry Streets), both Lutheran, for worship.

The famed Lutheran minister Henry Melchior Muhlenberg (1711–1787) is shown to have often visited Kensington to marry residents, minister to the sick, baptize children, bury the dead or even simply to socialize with friends.

Muhlenberg was born in Einbeck, Hanover, and was ordained by the Leipzig Consistory in 1739. He immigrated to America and eventually arrived in Philadelphia in 1742. He served a number of churches in Pennsylvania, including those in Philadelphia.

The Journals of Henry Melchior Muhlenberg were published by the Evangelical Lutheran Ministerium of Pennsylvania and Adjacent States and the Muhlenberg Press back in 1942. Muhlenberg's journals first record him visiting Kensington on October 9, 1762, when he was "summoned to Kensington to baptize Kriechenmeyer's sick little daughter."

Elizabeth Chevalier (1767, d. bef. 1794), the great-granddaughter of Kensington founder Anthony Palmer, married John Schaffer, whose sister was the wife of the Reverend Henry Muhlenberg's son, Frederick Augustus Conrad Muhlenberg (1750–1801), the very first Speaker of the U.S. House of Representatives.

When the nineteenth century arrived, there were still no churches in Kensington. The area contained only two grocery stores and six taverns, or "country inns." There were no paved streets, nor were there sidewalks. When the winter frost would leave, there would often be three- to four-foot ditches along Richmond Street, between Palmer and Columbia, and out to the river. The ditches acted as conduits to convey the melting snow to the river. There was not a row of houses in Kensington. In a few places, there may have been two or three buildings that were joined together, but mostly there were irregular gaps between single homes. Many of the homes were two and a half stories with gardens in front of them. Most residents owned their homes.

Many people were still going into Philadelphia for worship services. Some groups would meet at homes in the area, or, in the case of local Baptists, the foot of Bishop (later Vienna, now Berks) Street at the Delaware River (which had a natural sandy beach) became a popular place to be baptized.

While the Baptists were being baptized in the river and the Lutherans were going into town to Saint Michael's or Zion, Kensington's Methodists were going into town to Saint George's Church, at 4th and New (just below Vine) Streets. In bad weather they may have stopped at Zoar Church, at Brown above 4th Street, and worshipped with the African Americans there.

In 1801, the Kensington Methodists began meeting as the "Class at Kensington," with John Hewson, the Revolutionary War hero, as leader. Among this class were Hewson's wife Zebiah, his daughter-in-law Ann Hewson and several members of the Jones family, Edward, John and Anthony. The group first started to meet on what was called "Sheep Hill," which was said to be at the northwest corner of Queen (Richmond) and Crown (Crease) Streets. Sheep Hill was supposed to have extended from this intersection to about where 221 Richmond Street was located, or about halfway down the block to Shackamaxon Street. "Sheep Hill" had a double, two-story brick house, painted yellow, standing twenty feet back from the street and reached by climbing a flight of steps resting against the bank on Richmond Street.

It was not uncommon at this point in history for the Methodists to have rocks thrown through the windows by local rowdies.

By 1804, in good weather, the Methodists of Kensington were preaching under "the shade of the Penn Treaty Tree," which stood nearby at what is today's Penn Treaty Park. Logs of the local shipyard served as benches. In 1809, the Kensington Society of Methodists founded the Kensington ME (Old Brick) Church, the first church established in Fishtown or Kensington, and after erecting a church building on a lot they purchased at Richmond and Marlborough Streets, Kensingtonians finally had a place to worship.

THE BIBLE CHRISTIAN CHURCH AND THE FOUNDING OF THE VEGETARIAN MOVEMENT

Be not among winebibbers, and riotous eaters of flesh.
—Proverbs 23:20

Kensington was the birthplace of the American vegetarian movement. It sounds rather odd, but it is most definitely true. Verses from the Bible, such as the above, convinced a group of Englishmen to devote their lives to both vegetarianism and the Bible and, at the same time, blend the history of the vegetarian movement in America to our very own Kensington's history.

The story starts with the Reverend William Metcalfe, who was influenced by the teachings of William Cowherd, a breakaway minister of the English church. He began preaching strict adherence to the Bible, requiring members to proclaim themselves as "Bible Christians," as well as practice vegetarianism and abstinence from intoxicating liquors.

Metcalfe became a minister and took charge of a small church in Salford, England, based on Cowherd's principles. He and his congregation were enthused with the prospects of religious freedom offered by America. With his flock of vegetarians, Metcalfe immigrated to Philadelphia in 1817.

During the first few years in Philadelphia, there was apprehension by other denominations toward Metcalfe's Bible Christians, who were seen as odd, with most folks focused on their vegetarianism. Over time, however, "as individuals and also as an organization, they gradually acquired the respect and esteem of the educated and enlightened portion of the community... and frequently received most favorable comment in the public Press."

It took a while to get organized, but eventually the first Bible Christian Church was established on the west side of 3rd Street, above Girard Avenue, in about the middle of the block. An old frame schoolhouse was removed to the plot of ground purchased by the church. It stood from 1823 to 1844. This was replaced with a large brick structure built in 1845 and lasting until 1890, when the church sold the property.

For the first ten years in Philadelphia, William Metcalfe labored, until finally, in 1830, he caught the interest of Dr. Sylvester Graham, the famed graham cracker developer and diet reformer, who was interested in the Bible Christian's principles of vegetarianism and abstinence from alcohol. At the same time, Metcalfe began a correspondence with Dr. William A. Alcott, who also at that time publicly declared his conviction for vegetarianism. Alcott converted his cousin Bronson Alcott (father of Louisa May Alcott and

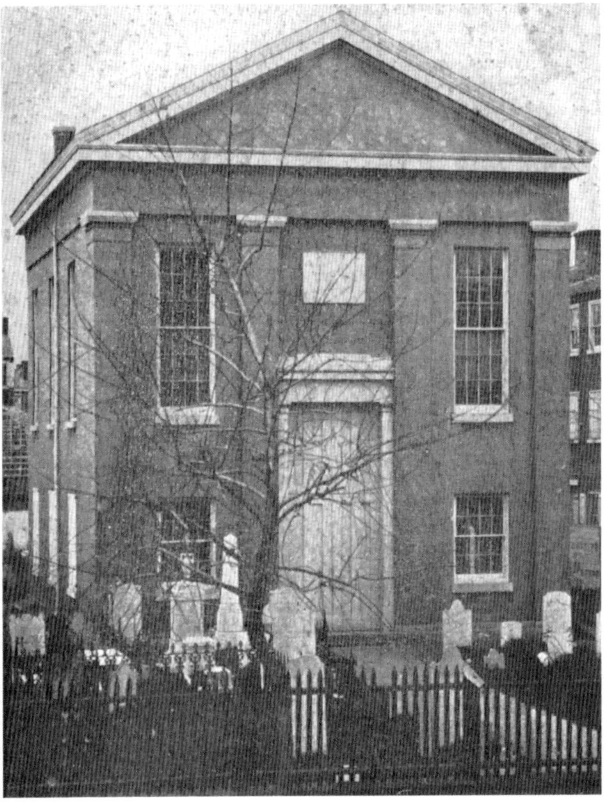

The Bible Christian Church was a vegetarian church built in 1845 on the west side of 3rd Street, above Girard. Burk's slaughterhouse was built upon the site of church.

an inspiration to the Transcendentalist movement) to vegetarianism as early as 1835, and thus there were three influential voices of the day in agreement with Metcalfe's ideas.

It is said that Metcalfe had an enormous influence over Graham, and Graham, in turn, would later have an enormous influence over John Harvey Kellogg, of breakfast cereal fame. Kellogg, while already an adherent to vegetarianism, became convinced by Graham's views on dieting and this helped to turn Kellogg's mind to food reform. Thus, Kellogg cereals and graham crackers are today's healthy testaments to these early years of the vegetarian movement in Kensington.

Later, in the 1840s, Metcalfe, in corresponding with his counterparts in America, helped to organize the first vegetarian convention in America. The minister from Kensington was elected president. Out of this convention the Vegetarian Society was formed. The Kensington Bible Christian Church was the host for the society's fifth annual meeting. At this fifth convention, there were said to be 150 participants that feasted on a vegetarian banquet underneath a banner that proclaimed:

And God said, Behold, I have given you every herb seed, which is upon the face of all the earth, and every tree, in the which is the fruit of a tree yielding seed; to you it shall be for meat.

—Genesis 1:29

Metcalfe, the church's founder and minister for the first forty-five years (1817–1862), was succeeded at his death by his son Joseph Metcalfe, who died suddenly after only five years (1862–1867) as head of the church. Dr. William Taylor, the grandson of William Metcalfe, became minister for a short time (1868–1873), and afterward was replaced by a longtime vegetarian advocate, the Reverend Henry S. Clubb, who presided over the church from 1876 until his death in 1921.

It was during Clubb's tenure that the church moved from Kensington to a new church on Park Avenue, south of Berks Street. The church lasted there from 1891 to 1916, before finally removing to Clubb's home at 1023 Foulkrod Street, in the Northwood section of Frankford, where a number of the members of the church had relocated over the years.

For sixty-eight years the Bible Christian Church held services at their church in Kensington. Oddly enough, that sacred ground of the vegetarian movement in America was purchased by Burk Brothers and, much like the early tradition of the Catholic Church, which built churches on ancient pagan sites, Burks built their slaughterhouse for the butchering of meats on top of the old Bible Christian Church's sacred ground.

Saint Michael's Church 175th Anniversary

On Sunday, September 24, 2006, Cardinal Justin Rigali visited Saint Michael's Church, at 2nd and Jefferson Streets, as part of the yearlong celebration of the 175th anniversary of Saint Michael's Parish and Church.

Saint Michael's is the oldest Catholic Church in Kensington or Fishtown. Irish Catholics founded the church when many of them were newly arrived immigrants. They were hand weavers who came to work in the emerging textile mill district that would eventually dominate the Kensington area. Of the five Irish clusters in nineteenth-century Philadelphia, Kensington's Irish were considered the most skilled. Places like Southwark, Moyamensing, Passyunk and Spring Garden all had large Irish immigrant concentrations, but in those areas, many of the Irish were forced to work unskilled jobs as laborers, carters and coal heavers.

Founded in April 1831, Saint Michael's was established eleven years before Saint Peter's, the next oldest Catholic Church in the general Kensington area, founded in 1842. Saint Peter's, a German Catholic Church, sits on the western bank of the old Cohocksink Creek, the former border of the then self-governing districts of Kensington and Northern Liberties. Many members of this church lived in Kensington (including my own mother's family, who had lived in Kensington since the 1840s), but went to church at Saint Peter's because they were German, not Irish. Otherwise, they would have gone to Saint Michael's.

Saint Anne's, the third oldest church in the area, was not founded until July 1845. Saint Anne's would be the last church built in Kensington until after the Civil War. After the war, Kensington saw Saint Edward the Confessor being built in 1865, followed by Saint Boniface (German, 1866), Immaculate Conception (1869), Visitation Blessed Virgin Mary (BVM) (1873), Saint Laurentius (Polish, 1882) and finally Holy Name in 1905.

Not long ago, I had the opportunity to do some research that was indirectly related to Saint Michael's Church. I was researching the history of a house located on the 400 block of Master Street, and it turned out that the land was once owned by one of Kensington's richest men, Hugh Clarke. Clarke was the famous alderman who played such a big role in the anti–Irish Catholic riots of May 1844, which resulted in the Know-Nothings (Nativists) torching Saint Michael's Church. Being one of the leaders of the Irish Catholics, Clarke's house was sacked and burned during the riots, as was his brother Patrick's, whose property was also at 4th and Master Streets.

Clarke bought the property from Turner Camac, the husband of Sarah Masters, who was the daughter of William Masters, hence today's Master Street. Sarah and her sister Mary, wife of Richard Penn, grandson of William Penn, inherited their father's estate. The Masters estate made up most of what is South Kensington today, including the land on which Saint Michael's Church sits. It was through Turner Camac that the Catholic Church appears to have acquired the land to build Saint Michael's.

Much has been written about Saint Michael's history, and for those not familiar with this church's grand history, you can visit the church's website (http://www.saintmichael.catholicweb.com/) to learn of the "Awful Riots" against the Irish Catholics, the great train wreck of 1856 and the church's connection to the Sisters of Charity BVM and the Sisters of Saint Joseph.

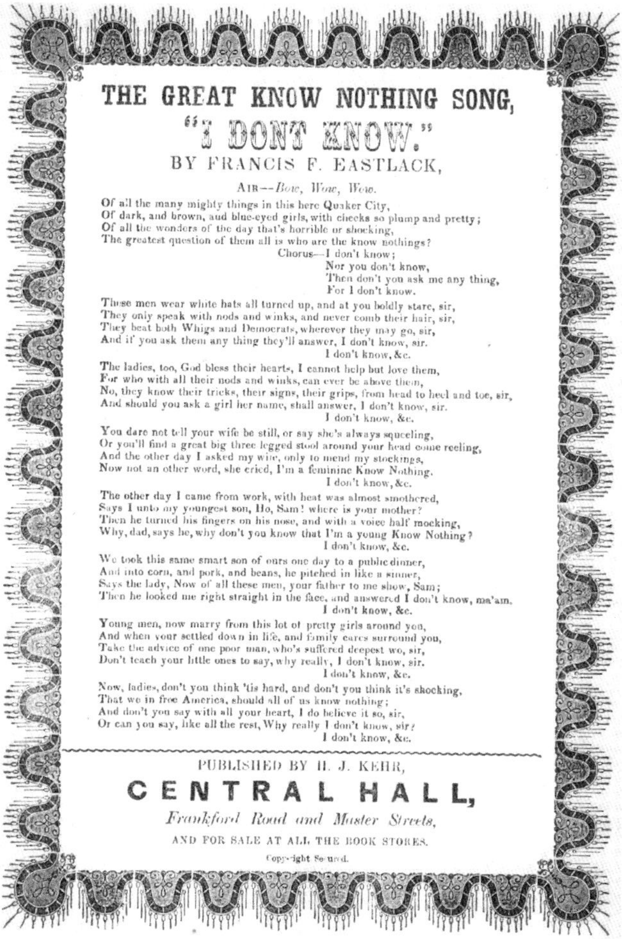

THE GREAT KNOW NOTHING SONG,

"I DONT KNOW."

BY FRANCIS F. EASTLACK,

AIR—*Bow, Wow, Wow.*

Of all the many mighty things in this here Quaker City,
Of dark, and brown, aud blue-eyed girls, with cheeks so plump and pretty;
Of all the wonders of the day that's horrible or shocking,
The greatest question of them all is who are the know nothings?
Chorus—I don't know;
Nor you don't know,
Then don't you ask me any thing,
For I don't know.

These men wear white hats all turned up, and at you boldly stare, sir,
They only speak with nods and winks, and never comb their hair, sir,
They beat both Whigs and Democrats, wherever they may go, sir,
And if you ask them any thing they'll answer, I don't know, sir.
I don't know, &c.

The ladies, too, God bless their hearts, I cannot help but love them,
For who with all their nods and winks, can ever be above them,
No, they know their tricks, their signs, their grips, from head to heel and toe, sir,
And should you ask a girl her name, shall answer, I don't know, sir.
I don't know, &c.

You dare not tell your wife be still, or say she's always squeeling,
Or you'll find a great big three legged stool around your head come reeling,
And the other day I asked my wife, only to mend my stockings,
Now not an other word, she cried, I'm a feminine Know Nothing.
I don't know, &c.

The other day I came from work, with heat was almost smothered,
Says I unto my youngest son, Ho, Sam! where is your mother?
Then he turned his fingers on his nose, and with a voice half mocking,
Why, dad, says he, why don't you know that I'm a young Know Nothing?
I don't know, &c.

We took this same smart son of ours one day to a public dinner,
And into corn, and pork, and beans, he pitched in like a sinner,
Says the lady, Now of all these men, your father to me show, Sam;
Then he looked me right straight in the face, and answered I don't know, ma'am.
I don't know, &c.

Young men, now marry from this lot of pretty girls around you,
And when your settled down in life, and family cares surround you,
Take the advice of one poor man, who's suffered deepest wo, sir,
Don't teach your little ones to say, why really, I don't know, sir.
I don't know, &c.

Now, ladies, don't you think 'tis hard, and don't you think it's shocking,
That we in free America, should all of us know nothing;
And don't you say with all your heart, I do believe it so, sir,
Or can you say, like all the rest, Why really I don't know, sir?
I don't know, &c.

PUBLISHED BY H. J. KEHR,

CENTRAL HALL,

Frankford Road and Master Streets,

AND FOR SALE AT ALL THE BOOK STORES.

Copyright Secured.

A Know-Nothing Party (Nativists) song sheet published in Kensington at the time of the anti-Irish Catholic riots in Kensington in 1844.

My own website also has information on the riots, as well as links where you can read, in full, the actual contemporary reports of the riots (www.kennethwmilano.com).

The folks at Saint Michael's worked hard all year to celebrate their 175th anniversary and, in the process, they formed a committee with the hopes of publishing a new history of the church. The committee was made up of Father Herbert Sperger, Brother Joe Grabenstein (archivist at LaSalle University), Gerry Burns, Kathleen Chorlton, Tom and Ray Lederer and Marge McTear (all of whose families have been involved with Saint Michael's for years, dating back to 1831). If you have any personal Saint Michael's stories to share, they would be very happy to hear from you. Pictures or other ephemeral items would also be of interest.

THE YELLOW FEVER COMES TO KENSINGTON

The yellow fever has a long history in Philadelphia. There were eleven outbreaks of the epidemic between 1780 and 1820, with none worse than the outbreak of 1793. The yellow fever was a virus with a three- to four-day incubation period. First came a fever, then muscle pain, particularly in the back, followed by headaches, shivers and a loss of appetite. Nausea and vomiting began, and the fever got worse. After three or four days, some improved and got better; however, a large percentage did not and they entered a toxic phase, which lasted about a day. The fever reappeared, affecting various systems in the body, and the victim became jaundiced, hence the name yellow fever. Abdominal pain and vomiting would continue, and bleeding might occur from the mouth, nose, eyes and stomach. Once this happened, blood appeared in the vomit and feces, and kidney functions deteriorated. The afflicted would die within fourteen days.

In each successive wave of the disease, Philadelphia health officials came to understand it better and drew up a list of recommendations to rid the city of various hazards that helped the disease spread, such as making alterations in cleansing the streets and alleys and forcing owners to pave alleys that led to public streets. Since many of the outbreaks were introduced to the city by ships coming into port, no wharf was to be "built unless the dock on either side be so deep as to be covered by water at low tide." Wharves were also to be paved and cleansed as the streets.

One recommendation was that no tavern should be granted a license or renewed, in any part of the city, unless the lot had sufficient space outside of the house for a privy. There was also a recommendation that no new tavern licenses be granted for any houses east of Front Street to the Delaware River, the reason being that "our summer pestilence has generally commenced and raged with the greatest violence within those limits, where, from the confined and filthy character of the localities, the exciting causes of fever arising from intemperate drinking would multiply victims to this disease."

In the outbreak of 1793, the yellow fever was said to have caused 4,044 deaths in Philadelphia. The census of 1790 gave the population of Philadelphia at that time as 28,522. If you included the population of Northern Liberties Township and Southwark, the total population for the metropolitan area would have been about 44,000, which means about 10 percent of the city was wiped out. Compared to the population of

Philadelphia today, reported to be about 1.4 million people, it would be equivalent to over 100,000 people dying in four months.

The 1793 yellow fever started slowly in August, with the death of 325 people. It increased dramatically in September, killing 1,442 people. It got worse in October when 1,976 individuals died, before finally subsiding when the cold weather started to set in. In November there were only 118 deaths.

In the federal census of 1790, Northern Liberties Township was listed as the sixth largest population center in all of America, behind New York, Philadelphia, Boston, Charleston and Baltimore. At that time, the Northern Liberties Township included everything north of Vine Street between the Delaware and Schuylkill Rivers, with the northern boundary being roughly Frankford and Wingohocking Creeks and Township Line.

In 1793, Northern Liberties Township reportedly had 543 deaths from the fever. Most, if not all, of these deaths were in today's Northern Liberties, Kensington and Fishtown neighborhoods, as the rest of the Northern Liberties Township was mostly unsettled.

From August to November of 1793 there were at least 169 burials at Kensington's Palmer Cemetery, all attributed to yellow fever. In a four-day period in September there were 31 burials. In 1793, there were no churches in Kensington, and since many of the cemeteries were attached to churches, many other Kensingtonians in all likelihood died from the fever and were buried at their church's burial ground, outside of the area.

One Kensington shipwright buried sixteen members of his own family in 1793. A blacksmith lost ten out of his seventeen journeymen; another lost all thirteen employees.

The outbreak in Kensington was attributed to Elizabeth Hill, the wife of Jacob Hill, one of the original fishermen of Fishtown. She is said to have contracted the disease when she was sailing near the infected wharves in Philadelphia. In all likelihood, she was probably transporting fish to sell at the fish market at Front and Market Streets, something many fishmonger wives of Fishtown so often did.

NORRIS SQUARE

HOME OF DR. KELLY'S KENSINGTON HOSPITAL FOR WOMEN, SAINT BONIFACE CHURCH AND THE KENSINGTON TUBERCULOSIS DISPENSARY

In the late nineteenth and early twentieth centuries, Kensington's Norris Square area was considered a prestigious address. The block-sized park was set aside by the Norris family, owners of the famed Fairhill estate. The Norris family allowed the Fairhill estate to be incorporated into the District of Kensington in 1848, at the time when Kensington was still a self-governing district. However, part of the agreement was that Norris Square would be kept as a green public space, to be enjoyed by future residents.

As the area around Norris Square developed, with a nice park already in place, large townhouses were built on the streets bordering the park. The square (Diamond Street on the south, Susquehanna Avenue on the north, Howard Street on the east and Hancock Street on the west) attracted a number of local wealthy families.

The Bromley carpet mill family, the Harbison dairy family and the Firth brothers, local dye manufacturers, were some of the families that inhabited the homes around the square in the nineteenth century. It was a short walk to the large Kensington businesses that were owned and operated by these families.

One interesting chapter of the Norris Square story is an individual by the name of Dr. Howard Atwood Kelly. Kelly was born in 1858, the son of Henry Kuhl Kelly. His father was a native Philadelphian who had a distinguished Civil War career, the high point of which was his presence at Appomattox Court House, where he assisted in receiving the Confederate arms and colors when General Lee surrendered in 1865.

Dr. Kelly's paternal grandmother, Margaret Kuhl, was the granddaughter of Michael Hillegas II and Henrietta Boude. Interestingly enough, both the Hillegas and Boude families were early landowners in Kensington, having purchased property from Anthony Palmer when he first set up his town in the 1730s.

Dr. Kelly attended Faires' Classical Institute, and afterward, the University of Pennsylvania, where he studied the classics and from which he graduated in 1877. He then entered the medical school at the University of Pennsylvania, taking his medical degree in 1882.

After a residency (1882–83) at Kensington's Episcopal Hospital at Front Street and Lehigh Avenue, he decided to stay in the area and began a practice among Kensington's millworkers. In about the year 1883, he "defied tradition" and established "his" private hospital, the Kensington Hospital for Women, the first women-only hospital in Philadelphia.

Such medical luminaries as William Osler, D. Hayes Agnew and Horatio Wood came to Kensington Women's Hospital as consultants. The Kensington Women's Hospital incorporated four years later and became a large and flourishing institution.

While in Kensington, Kelly lived for a time at 2516 North Front Street. The hospital that he founded was located at 130–136 Diamond Street, on the south side of Norris Square, and had a hundred-bed capacity, offering surgical, obstetrical, X-ray, outpatient, laboratory and gynecological services. It also had associated with it a nurses' training school, which was accredited and organized in 1888.

Dr. Kelly originally organized the Kensington Hospital for Women in February 1883. At first, it was located at 2821 "C" Street, in the house of Mrs. Kate Wood, on whom Kelly had previously operated. Mrs. Wood helped Kelly look after his patients, which consisted of three women when he first began. His success was almost immediate, as this was Philadelphia's first hospital that was devoted exclusively to the care of women.

Kelly was forced to move to larger quarters three times, once in 1885 and then again in 1886, until finally he moved to the Diamond Street location in 1890. The hospital was incorporated that year, with the charter having been granted back in 1887.

Kelly sat on the original board of directors for the hospital, with another local fellow by the name of John B. Stetson. Stetson, of course, is known the world over as the founder of the Kensington hat-making firm that created "the hat that won the west."

After founding the hospital, securing a charter and a large enough facility and helping to set up its incorporation, Kelly felt confident enough to let the hospital grow on its own. It was at this point that Kelly resigned and moved on to Johns Hopkins Hospital and University at Baltimore, Maryland, where his fame continued and he established himself as a leading authority in gynecology and surgery.

Besides Kelly, there were other famous surgeons and doctors associated with the Kensington Hospital for Women, including William W. Keen (1837–1932), who in 1887, only a couple of blocks away at Saint Mary's Hospital (later Neumann Medical Center), performed the first successful removal of a brain tumor in the United States. Earlier, in 1876, also at Saint Mary's, Keen was the first surgeon in Philadelphia to adopt Lister's principles of antisepsis, which was a carbolic acid wash and disinfectant that helped stop infections during surgery.

Dr. Kelly's desire to study gynecology took him to Europe on several occasions, to the famous medical schools of England, Scotland, France and Germany. When he returned, he took a position as associate professor of obstetrics at the University of Pennsylvania for the years 1888–89, before moving on to Johns Hopkins University.

Kelly joined the faculty of the then-famed Johns Hopkins University in Baltimore, in association with the equally famous William Osler, who had recruited him. He held the chair of gynecology and obstetrics until 1899, when he gave up obstetrics to continue as professor of gynecology. He became emeritus professor in 1919 and was associated with Johns Hopkins until his death in 1943. Kelly also had a large private practice that he attended.

During the course of his life, Dr. Kelly became a leading world authority in operative and medical gynecology, as well as abdominal surgery. He published numerous books and articles upon various scientific, surgical and medical topics, and helped to establish gynecology as a specialty in the field of medicine.

Besides the famed Dr. Howard Atwood Kelly's Kensington Women's Hospital being on Norris Square, Saint Boniface Church also helped to anchor the south side of the park. The church actually predated Kelly's hospital, having been founded in 1866.

Saint Boniface was a German Catholic church founded by the Redemptorist order of priests, as was the nearby Saint Peter's Church at 5th and Girard, the home of the shrine of Saint John Neumann. The two churches administered to the numerous German Catholic immigrants in the area who came mainly from Bavaria and Baden-Wurtemberg, that southwest corner of Germany long known to have never strayed from the Catholic faith.

Saint Boniface was closed in 2006, but key elements of the liturgical art were saved and are to be relocated to Blessed Teresa of Calcutta Roman Catholic Church in Limerick Township, Pennsylvania. Included are the gothic marble center altar, the grand pipe organ surround, the detailed confessionals, the elaborate baptismal font and the entire back wall of the church.

While these two institutions (Kensington Women's Hospital and Saint Boniface Church) were on the south side of the square, the north side of the square once housed the Kensington Dispensary for the Treatment of Tuberculosis. While uncommon today, the early twentieth century saw many cases of tuberculosis.

The dispensary was founded in 1905 by a group of local German Lutheran women. These women tended to be the wives of the local German

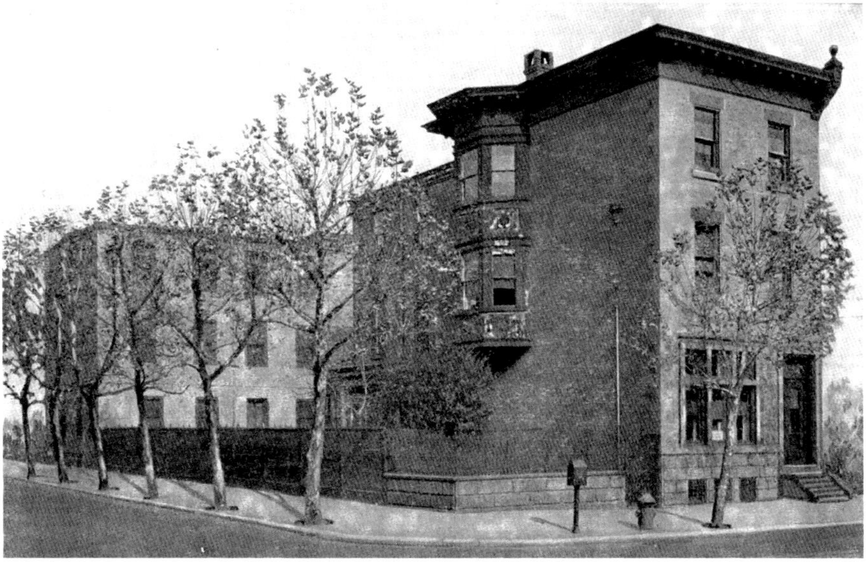

The Kensington Tuberculosis Dispensary, on Norris Square, at the corner of Hancock Street and Susquehanna Avenue, circa 1930, was founded by a group of Lutheran women.

businessmen and manufacturers. The dispensary was founded for "the purpose of assisting the suffering from Tuberculosis." At first, it was located on the southwest corner of Trenton and Susquehanna Avenues. In 1908, it moved to the north side of Norris Square, on the corner of Hancock Street and Susquehanna Avenue, where it remained until at least 1937.

In 1937, Mrs. Theodore C. Schoenhut was president and Miss Caroline Schoenhut was on the board of managers. The Schoenhut family, founders of Kensington's world famous Schoenhut Toy Company, seems to have taken an active interest in this institution, as four members of the family were listed as life members. The family's toy factory was located where today's Hackett School's schoolyard sits (southeast corner of Sepviva and Hagert Streets), and it produced some of the best toys in the world at that time.

In order to raise the funds for the dispensary, fourteen women's auxiliaries were set up around the city (two in Kensington), with membership dues and fundraising activities going to support the dispensary. The group had two thousand members as well as corporate and business sponsors.

One can imagine a very densely populated factory district like Kensington with residents sometimes living in substandard housing conditions. These conditions created a nice breeding ground for a disease like tuberculosis. During its first twenty-five years (1905–1930), the Kensington Dispensary gave over 90,000 treatments, with another 7,400 in home treatments. They also gave away close to 175,000 quarts of milk.

If a person were too ill to come into the dispensary, a physician was available for home visits. Nurses were also available to train the family in how to deal with the tuberculosis patient. Dr. Louis Herman, another Norris Square resident, was the dentist for the dispensary.

Later, in 1913, the Kensington Dispensary offered a "Preventorium," called River Crest, located at Mount Clare, Pennsylvania. At this facility, children with tuberculosis, or children whose parents had tuberculosis, were given the opportunity for "medical supervision, fresh air, nourishing food" and "kindly care," all of which helped to rebuild the "wasted tissue" and helped in "gaining weight" and all around "happy improvements." The facility allowed the tuberculosis patients to be taken out of the crowded, polluted environment of the factory district so that they might have a better chance of recovery.

With Kelly's Kensington Women's Hospital and the Kensington Dispensary, the Norris Square neighborhood sure seems to have had its healthcare needs met.

PART VI

SOME KENSINGTON BIOGRAPHIES

THOMAS MORAN

AMERICAN LANDSCAPE PAINTER

With the gentrification of Fishtown and parts of Kensington, the influx of artisans into the communities has been greatly increasing. On May 6, 2006, Kensington was treated to, for the first time, its very own Annual Arts Festival, which took place on Trenton Avenue, south of Dauphin Street. I had the opportunity to visit the Arts Festival. It was well attended, had live music and numerous vendors, as well as good food to eat while you strolled along.

It was all rather strange to this lifelong resident, seeing the younger generation of tattooed ladies and pierced men walking up and down Trenton Avenue, milling about and generally making themselves comfortable sitting on the ground. My kids loved it—they got free balloons shaped liked swords—and I was quite pleased with the influx of new neighbors and the energy they bring. I guess those young Fishtown girls with homemade tattoos, the scourge of the city when I was a youth, are now seen as trendsetters!

As might be expected, artists are not new to Kensington; they might just look a bit different today. My mother's brother, Martin Kaelin (Sr.), had been a painter and art teacher his whole life. He grew up on the 1100 block of Germantown Avenue from the late 1920s thru the 1950s. His fascination with New Orleans, early brass bands and street life were at the heart of his paintings and brought him into contact with many of the jazz greats of New Orleans. (He would eventually count among his personal friends Louis Armstrong, Al Hirt and the Jaffes, founders of Preservation Hall, to name a few.)

If we took a trip back to the nineteenth century, we would find that Kensington was home to one of America's most famous landscape artists, the painter Thomas Moran (1837–1926), who spent his formative years here.

Born in England, Moran's parents immigrated to Philadelphia in 1844 when Thomas was a young boy. His father, Thomas Moran Sr., was a handloom weaver, and Kensington had a reputation for handloom weaving, so it was a natural draw for him.

Starting out near 4th and Master Streets in 1844, the Moran family had at least a twenty-five-year relationship with Kensington. From 4th and Master in the 1840s, in 1851 the Morans were living on 5th Street, below Jefferson, where they had been enumerated in Kensington's Third Ward in the 1850 census.

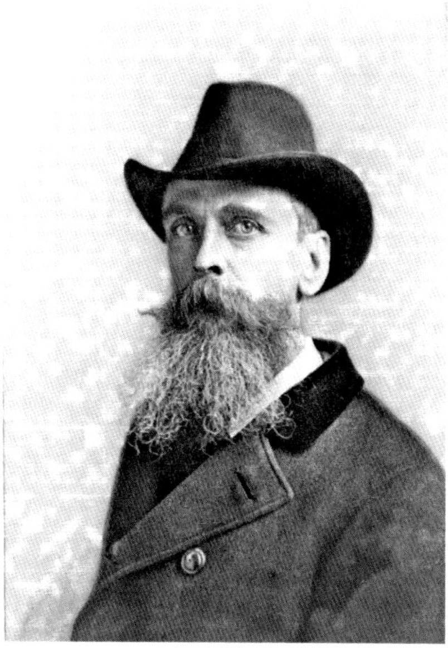

Thomas Moran, a famous landscape painter, lived as a youth at 4th and Master Streets. *Courtesy of the Library of Congress, Prints & Photographs Division, circa 1890s.*

During the Civil War years of 1861 to 1864, Edward Moran, Thomas's older brother and also an artist, was listed as living at 915 East Sergeant Street. Sergeant Street in 1861 is described as being located "west from Frankford Avenue above Cumberland Street." The 900 block of Sergeant Street would presumably be somewhere between Frankford and Kensington Avenues. The numbering system in the 1860s was different than what it is today. It would appear that Edward Moran was enumerated in the 1860 census in the Tenth Ward, Eastern District, but moved back to Kensington the following year and stayed there during the war years.

Edward's more famous brother, Thomas Moran, and his other siblings and parents were living at 927 North 11th Street in 1861, before moving to the 8th and Coates (Fairmount) Street area in 1862, an area where they stayed at least until Edward Moran left Kensington and joined them there by 1870. By the 1870 census, it appears that all of the Moran family members were out of Kensington and had moved closer to town, to the Northern Liberties and East Popular areas, or downtown, where the Moran boys would eventually set up studios along the more prominent streets in downtown Philadelphia.

Thomas Moran's early education took place in Kensington. He came to America at about the age of seven and did not start his career in art until about the age of fifteen, when he became apprenticed to an engraver. Starting out at 4th and Master in an industrial setting and then becoming America's most famous landscape painter seems odd, but perhaps it was the drudgery of the congested and polluted neighborhood that made Moran seek solitude and beauty in nature.

Moran's real reputation took hold after he took a number of trips to paint the landscapes of the American West, mostly done while on government surveying expeditions. One of his paintings entitled *The Grand Canyon of the Yellowstone* hangs at the Capitol Building in Washington, D.C., along with a companion piece of his titled, *The Chasm of the Colorado*. His paintings of the Western United States fascinated the people back East. The pictures were large, grand and brilliant with color. Moran's paintings of Yellowstone were said to be responsible for convincing Congress and President Ulysses S. Grant to lay aside this area as America's very first national park.

I previously wrote about Kensington's involvement in the founding of the vegetarian movement in America, and this week I'm writing about Kensington and the founding of the American park system. Is there no end to the energies of our residents!

Albert C. Barnes

Inventor and Art Collector

One of Fishtown's most famous native sons in the art world was Albert C. Barnes, who built one of the best art collections in the world. Barnes was also famous for his temperament, and it is quite possible that the famous chip on his shoulder directed toward the "art establishment," a chip as famous as his collection, developed while growing up on the streets of Fishtown.

His father was John Jesse Barnes, of Irish background, whose family is said to have immigrated to Pennsylvania in colonial times. He was a butcher in his youth, and it is said that he worked alongside the famous transportation magnate Peter A.B. Widener, before Widener made his wealth in that field.

When the Civil War broke out Barnes's father enlisted in the Eighty-second Infantry Regiment of Pennsylvania Volunteers. During the battle of Cold Harbor, Virginia, he was wounded in his right arm. The wounds were so bad that he had to have the arm amputated.

Barnes's father collected his pension from the government, but he did not let a little thing like a lost arm get in the way of making a living. He became a one-armed postman.

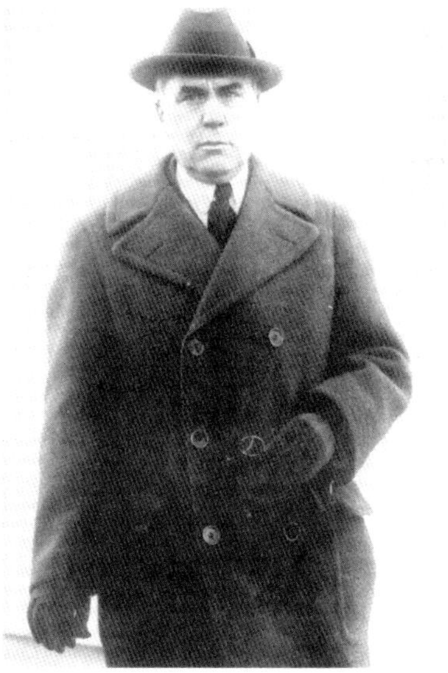

Dr. Albert C. Barnes spent the first ten years of his life growing up on the 1400 block of Wilt Street in Fishtown.

Barnes's father met and married Lydia A. Schafer and together they had four children, all boys.

Albert C. Barnes was born on January 2, 1872, in a small house on today's 1400 block of Wilt Street, between Memphis and Gaul Streets. In 1872, Wilt Street was still known as Cork Street and the Barnes family lived at 1466 Cork, a two-story brick home on a row house block.

Barnes spent the first ten years of his life growing up in Fishtown, which at that time was pretty much the way it is today. Back then (1870s), the residents would have been made up of mostly the English, Scots-Irish and Irish, with some Germans. From Fishtown, at the age of ten years old, Albert C. Barnes moved with his family to "the Neck," a rather nasty area of deep–South Philadelphia, where Barnes was forced to learn to box to get respect from the neighborhood kids.

After three years in the Neck, the Barnes family moved to the 1300 block of Tasker Street, also in South Philadelphia, where, at thirteen years old, Barnes was accepted into Central High School, which at that time still gave bachelor's of arts and bachelor's of science degrees to its graduates. Barnes's graduating class included the Ashcan painters John Sloan and William Glackens, whom he would become better friends with in later life.

After Central High, Barnes attended the University of Pennsylvania, getting his MD degree in 1892. At this point, Barnes began to make a number of trips to Germany, the leading country in the sciences and pharmacology at that time. There, he enrolled at Heidelberg in courses on therapeutics and pharmacology.

After returning to America, Barnes went into business with Herman Hille, whom he had met in Germany, using a makeshift laboratory in an old stable at 13th and Spruce Streets in downtown Philadelphia. Soon, Barnes perfected his discovery of Argyrol, a "silver protein compound that he hoped would be more antiseptic, and less caustic, than silver nitrate," which was then being used for all sorts of ills.

Barnes's Argyrol became a huge success, and he became quite wealthy. Over time, Barnes became an avid collector of art, particularly Impressionist and post-Impressionist painters, at a time when they were not yet getting the recognition they would attract later in the century. His collection of paintings—in particular his Renoirs, Matisses, Cezannes and Picassos—number in the hundreds. He is also credited with "discovering" Soutine and Modigliani. His art collection is considered one of the finest collections in the world. Not bad for a kid from Wilt Street.

In addition, Barnes developed his own philosophy of aesthetics, which became the foundation for the Barnes School and Museum, run by his "rigid and controversial principles." His name is always associated with the adjectives "controversial" and "idiosyncratic," and it is said that he left "more ill will than any other single figure in American art." Gertrude Stein said of Barnes's art purchases, "He did literally wave his cheque book in the air."

Barnes died in a tragic car accident in 1951.

Barnes was a self-made millionaire with a Fishtown background. What appears to have upset the cultured classes the most about Barnes is that, like most working-class folks, he was not afraid to speak his mind—if he offended, he really didn't care.

W.C. FIELDS AND ED WYNN

ACTORS AND COMEDIANS

To show that Fishtown and Kensington were not all about industry and hard work, I am turning my eyes to two fellows, both with connections to the area, who happened to have been two of the funniest comedians known to America.

Claude William Dukenfield, also known as W.C. Fields, was born on January 29, 1880. One story states that he was born near 9th and Cambria

Streets, but the 1880 census shows his family living at 64th and Woodland when Fields was only four months old.

W.C. Fields was the oldest son of James Dukenfield and Katie Felton. His father made a living as a huckster, peddling produce.

His father was an English immigrant, whose parents first settled in Kensington, on Norris Street, just west of Front, in the late 1850s. W.C. Fields's grandfather, John Dukenfield, was a comb maker and had a very large family. Fields's father had at least seven brothers and two sisters.

James Dukenfield, Fields's father, served in the Pennsylvania Infantry during the American Civil War. On the 1890 Veterans Schedule Census, Fields's parents were living at 2803 Germantown, another stop before moving to Marshall Street, above Erie Avenue, where the family lived for a while.

It is stated that Fields's formal education stopped at the fourth grade. Early on, he became interested in vaudeville and the stage. H.M. Lorette, billed as the "Original Dancing Juggler," lived as a youth at 15th and Cumberland Streets and is said to have practiced with Fields when he was learning how to juggle.

Fields started at an amusement park on the Delaware River, and then worked a gig for a week at Plymouth Park, near Norristown. Lorette states that he helped Fields get a spot at the Fortesque Pavilion in Atlantic City, after which Fields met up with the Spencer Brothers, an Irish comedy group. He went with this group on a tour with a "Turkey Burlesque" show called *The Monte Carlo Girls*, where he met his wife Harriet Hughes, of New York, who was one of the chorus girls.

Fields married "Hattie" in 1900, and together they had a son, W.C. Fields Jr. However, Hattie refused to travel on the road with the boy, and it appears that may have been the end of the marriage. While the marriage soured, they never divorced and were still married at his death.

By the time he was a teenager, Fields began performing onstage, and at the turn of the century, the Keith Orpheum Circuit, a well-known vaudeville group, signed Fields. His pantomime and juggling acts took him all over the world, even playing before King Edward VII at Buckingham Palace.

W.C. Fields starred in the famous Ziegfield Follies for the 1915 edition, and oddly enough, that year he was teamed with a Kensington fellow named Isaiah Edwin Leopold, also known as Ed Wynn.

Ed Wynn was born in 1888 to Jewish immigrant parents. The family lived at their millinery business at 2518 Kensington Avenue, not too far from where W.C. Fields's father first lived when he came to America. Ed Wynn worked for his father selling hats, before eventually running away to seek his fame and fortune on the stage.

Ed Wynn became one of America's best-known funnymen, having not only starred in the Ziegfield Follies, but also boasting a successful vaudeville and Broadway career, as well as radio, television and film. He starred in a number of big-screen movies, including *The Diary of Ann Frank*, which won him an Academy Award nomination for best supporting actor in 1959. Wynn died in Beverly Hills, California, in 1966.

W.C. Fields was considered by many to be a comic genius, with some going so far as to say that he was "quite probably the funniest single individual America has ever produced." Besides his vaudeville and Broadway shows, Fields also made a number of films, both in the silent era and when the talkies emerged. Some of his most memorable films were done later in his career, including *My Little Chickadee* and *The Bank Dick*, both in 1940. *Never Give a Sucker an Even Break* in 1941 was his last feature-length film.

W.C. Fields died in 1946 in Los Angeles from "internal hemorrhage," complicated by dropsey. He was sixty-six years old.

Jack "Legs" Diamond

American Gangster

One local story that always interested me was the rumor that the notorious Jack "Legs" Diamond, the New York gangster, grew up in Kensington. This story had always circulated, but I never did find anyone that could tell me much more than "yeah, he was from this neighborhood, my uncle told me so."

The birth of Legs Diamond is a mystery. What most people who take an interest in criminal history say on the matter is that he was born in Philadelphia in or about the year 1897. Some say his real name was Jack Moran, others say it was John T. Nolan. Both groups are certain that he was born in Philadelphia and became involved in organized crime in New York after serving time in jail as a deserter during World War I. In New York, he made his name in the underworld by working with people like Arnold Rothstein and against people like Dutch Schultz, the predecessors to the Mafia.

Since the neighborhood story was that Legs Diamond came from my immediate area (Saint Anne's Parish), I decided to try and find evidence to prove it. I did this by conducting fairly thorough searches of the 1900 and

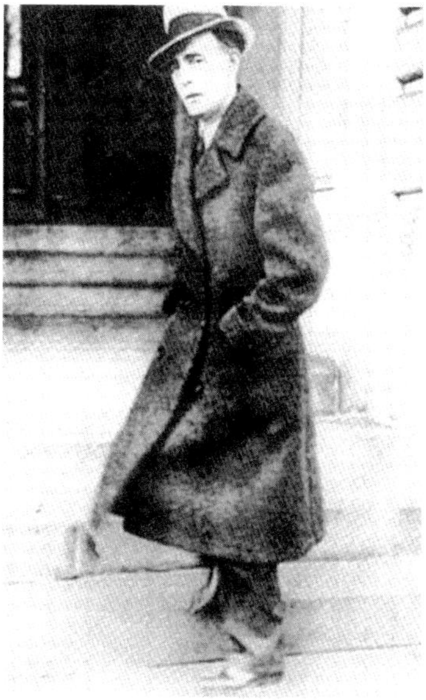

American gangster Jack "Legs" Diamond (1898–19??) once lived on the 2300 block of Albert Street and the 2100 block of East York Street.

1910 censuses for Philadelphia as a whole, and in particular the Thirty-first Ward.

There was no John/Jack Moran, nor John/Jack Nolan or John T. Nolan, listed that would have fit the birth year for Legs Diamond, even factoring in a cushion on each side of a couple of years. However, I did find that there was a John Diamond who lived in the neighborhood and was a close match with Legs Diamond's date of birth. In addition, I found that this John Diamond had the middle initial of "T," the same as the alias used by Legs Diamond (John T. Nolan) when he once went to Europe but was refused entry. I also found he had a younger brother Edward, which is a known fact for Legs Diamond.

In the 1900 census, the household of John Diamond Jr. (born January 1871) shows him to have been married for four years to Sarah (born February 1873). The couple had one child, John T. Diamond, born about July 1898. The family lived at 2336 Albert Street, at about Memphis Street, near Saint Anne's School.

The child named John is probably Jack "Legs" Diamond. His mother, Sarah Hart, was the daughter of Irish immigrants. John and his father were both listed as born in Pennsylvania. The elder John Diamond was working as a glass packer.

Also listed in the house was John Diamond's brother Thomas and sister Annie. His brother was a machinist; his sister worked in a hosiery mill. The last person in the house was John Jr.'s sister-in-law, Margaret C. Hart, which is how we find the probable maiden name of Legs Diamond's mother.

At this point, the name and age seemed to be good matches, particularly when there were no Morans or Nolans that matched. I next took a look at the 1910 census.

In the 1910 census, further evidence was found that would seem to indicate that this John T. Diamond might just be the right fellow. In the boardinghouse of Mary E. Sturn was found the family of John J. Diamond Jr. (Legs's supposed father). Mrs. Sturn's boardinghouse was located at 2157 East York Street, just west of Frankford Avenue. Mrs. Sturn was the divorced daughter of Irish immigrants, and besides her two teenage sons, she boarded the Diamond family and two other men who worked in the nearby textile mills.

In 1910, the Diamond family now consisted of only the father John J. Diamond, his son John and another son, Edward. Edward is listed as born about 1902. The father is listed as a widow. This 1910 census finding is very interesting, as it shows John T. having a younger brother Edward, which is a known fact for the gangster Legs Diamond. Edward Diamond left Philadelphia with Legs Diamond, and both of them pursued a life of crime in the Big Apple.

The information found in the 1900 and 1910 censuses is for the same Diamond family and would appear to show evidence that might be a very good starting point to make a case for Legs Diamond coming from Kensington. This sort of preliminary evidence would generally be followed up with searches for birth and death records, as well as other supporting evidence. It is said that Legs Diamond was a Catholic, so perhaps he was baptized at Saint Anne's.

The only real problem with this sort of project is: Do we really need/want to prove that another famous criminal came from our neighborhood?

EDWARD CORNER

MARINE MERCHANDISER AND PHILANTHROPIST

Recent research has shown that there was a Revolutionary War fort built by the British military on the site where Sugarhouse Casino proposes to build a casino. In order to get a better visual idea of just where that fort might have stood, I drove down to the Sugarhouse site and, after examining it and getting the information that I wanted, I turned to see the Edward Corner building across the street from the casino site.

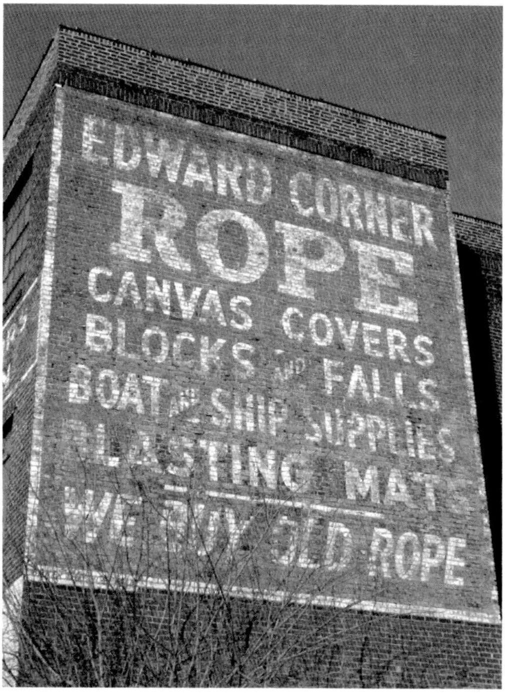

Edward Corner, the north corner of Delaware Avenue and Shackamaxon, provided a full range of supplies to the neighboring shipyards. *Courtesy Torben Jenk.*

On the northwest corner of Shackamaxon Street and Delaware Avenue, there stands a building by itself, one of the last vestiges of the great shipbuilding industry of Kensington (Fishtown), Edward L. Corner's Marine Merchandizing Warehouse. Corner, besides being a local businessman, was also widely known for his great philanthropy, and before this structure is either destroyed or turned into condominiums, I thought I would share a little of its history.

In the 1890 Philadelphia City Directory, the firm of Corner and Keighley was listed in the rag business at 1080 Beach Street. The proprietors were Edward Corner of 214 Allen Street and William J. Keighley of 159 Laurel Street. Edward L. Corner would have been only nineteen years old in 1890, so presumably this Edward Corner was the father of the later Edward L. Corner, whose business has long been closed, but still has the building standing at Shackamaxon and Delaware. An interesting stone in the building spells Shackamaxon as "Shakamaxon," without the "c."

By 1900, Edward Corner Sr. was listed as a junk dealer. He was born in England in 1840 and immigrated to America in 1859. Elizabeth Corner, Edward's wife, was born in Germany about 1850. She came to America in 1853. The couple married about 1870, the same year that Corner Sr. appears to have started his business.

Elizabeth was the mother of twelve children, of which six had died by the year 1900. In 1900, the Corners were living in a rented home at 214 Allen Street, with four of their children—three daughters and their son Edward L. Corner.

Edward L. Corner, the son of the above-mentioned Edward, was born in December 1872. In 1900, he was listed as a manager, presumably for the junk and rag business that his father started. Oddly enough, his parents' home on the 200 block of Allen Street was just a couple of doors away from the original 1844 home of the Kensington Soup Society, before it eventually moved to the Crease Street address.

Edward L. Corner would eventually become the longest running president of the Kensington Soup Society (1919–1955), leading the Soup Society through the worst economic depression in America's history, as well as World War II. Corner originally joined the board of managers of the Soup Society in 1906, serving the society for a full forty-nine years in many capacities, including as chairman of the hundredth-anniversary committee in 1944.

Edward Corner Sr. died sometime between 1900 and 1910. His wife Elizabeth took over the business. She moved to the 1300 block of Marlborough Street with three of her daughters, while her son Edward L. married in 1903 and moved out of his mother's home to start his own family.

Edward Jr. married a woman named Bessie and moved to a home on the 400 block of East Thompson Street, and by at least 1930, he moved to 1210 Columbia Avenue, to a home that he purchased. At this point, he had taken over his father's business and moved into other areas.

By the early twentieth century, Edward L. Corner was running a marine merchandise warehouse at 1100–1102 North Delaware Avenue, selling new and used rope, anchors and chains, canvas covers, boat supplies, blocks and falls and blasting mats.

The building that still stands was erected in 1921, as witnessed by the corner stone. Another marking has 1870, which is probably the date that his father first started the business. That earlier business of his father's was located at 1080 Beach Street, but it appears to have been obliterated when Delaware Avenue came through.

Edward L. Corner died on October 9, 1955. His family is supposed to have continued to own the property on Delaware Avenue until about 1960. Corner will be best known for his extreme generosity. There are still old-timers around that remember him.

FURTHER READING

All books are available at the Historical Society of Pennsylvania.

Alcock, Sarah. *A Brief History of the Revolution with a Sketch of the Life of John Hewson*. Philadelphia: Mrs. Sarah Alcock, 1843.

Catrambone, Jamie, and Harry C. Silcox, eds. *Kensington History: Stories and Memories*. Philadelphia: Brighton Press, 1996.

Cramp, Charles. *Memoirs of Churches in Old Kensington: Shipbuilders Paramount in Numbers and Influence in the "Old Brick" and "Chandler's"; Five Notable Vaughan Families*. Philadelphia: Public Ledger, 1909.

———. *Old Kensington District and Its Memories: Numerous European Settlers Before the English Occupation*. Philadelphia: n.p., 1909.

Cramp's Shipyard: The William Cramp & Son's Ship & Engine Building Company, 1830; the I.P. Morris Company, 1928; the Kensington Shipyard Company, 1900. Philadelphia: n.p., 1910.

Du Ponceau, Peter Stephen. *Memoir on the History of the Celebrated Treaty Made by William Penn*. Philadelphia: M'Carty & Davis, 1836.

Feind, Ernest, N. *A History of the First Presbyterian Church of Kensington*. Philadelphia: n.p., 1939.

Feldberg, Michael. *The Philadelphia Riots of 1844: A Study of Ethnic Conflict*. Westport, CT: Greenwood Press, 1975.

Gauer, David W. Vaughan. *Shipwrights of Kensington, Philadelphia: Their Van Hook & Norris Lineages and Combined Progeny*. Decorah, IA: Anundsen Pub. Co., 1982.

Grant, Karen, et al. *Fishtown—A Slice of Life: 300 Years in Philadelphia, 1682–1982*. Philadelphia: Fishtown Civic Association, 1982.

Heinrich, Thomas R. *Ships for the Seven Seas: Philadelphia Shipbuilding in the Age of Industrial Capitalism*. Baltimore: Johns Hopkins Press, 1997.

Jenk, Torben. Industrial Archaeology website. Workshop of the World. www.workshopoftheworld.com

Kensington: A City Within a City, Historical and Industrial Review. Philadelphia: Keighton Printing House, 1891.

McKearin, Helen. *Bottles, Flasks and Dr. Dyott*. New York: Crown Publishers, 1970.

Milano, Ken. Kensington History website. Encyclopaedia Kensingtoniana. www.kennethwmilano.com.

Molmer, Joseph S. *Kensington: From the Beginning to Consolidation*. N.p., 1854.

Needles, Samuel. *The Governor's Mill, and the Globe Mills, Philadelphia*. Philadelphia: Collins, 1884.

Remer, Rich. "Old Kensington." *Pennsylvania Legacies* 2, 2 (November 2002).

Scharf, J.T., and Thompson Westcott. *History of Philadelphia, 1609–1884*. Philadelphia: L.H. Everts, 1884.

Scranton, Philip. *Proprietary Capitalism: The Textile Manufacture at Philadelphia, 1800–1885*. New York: Cambridge University Press, 1983.

Seder, Jean. *Voices of Kensington: Vanishing Mills, Vanishing Neighborhoods*. Ardmore, PA: Whitmore Pub. Co, 1982.

Shane, Dennis J. *The History of the Kensington Burial Ground, Palmer Cemetery, Founded in 1732*. Philadelphia: Smith-Edwards-Dunlap Co., 1977.

Stutz, Bruce. *Natural Lives, Modern Times, People and Places of the Delaware River*. New York: Crown Publishers, 1992.

Swindells, William. *Annals of the Kensington Methodist Episcopal Church, Philadelphia*. Philadelphia: n.p., 1893.

Vaux, Roberts. *Memoir on the Locality of the Great Treaty Between William Penn and the Indian Natives in 1682*. Philadelphia: n.p., n.d.

Watson, John F. *Annals of Philadelphia, and Pennsylvania, in the Olden Time; Being a Collection of Memoirs, Anecdotes, and Incidents of the City and Its Inhabitants, and of the Earliest Settlements of the Inland Part of Pennsylvania*. Philadelphia: J.M. Stoddart & Co., 1877.